Endorsements

"This book is for leaders, managers and executives who want to get better, more predictable performance from every person."

Brian Tracy
How the Best Leaders Lead

"Exiting OZ ranks at the top of management leadership books. Start to finish, the book not only captivated my interest, it opened my eyes first to my own weaknesses as a leader and then to the weaknesses of people whom I coach and mentor. Exiting OZ at times made me very uncomfortable because it caused me to see, that as hard as I have worked over the years to be the level 5 leader Jim Collins describes, I am a Wizard in too many ways. No leader in any organization, public, private or non-profit, can read Exiting OZ without being motivated to rethink business as usual!"

Leonard Martin
Martin Management

"This work is a great analogy for the organizational malaise that is the clash between old world business and the expectations of a new generation of workers. With more and more workers looking for good leadership in today's modern organization, I am sure that even Dorothy would love to have read this book before going back to the land of OZ."

LaFaid Johnson Jr., PhD
Integrated Human Systems
Adjunct Professor, Argosy University

"Great leaders make great organizations. *Exiting OZ* is an excellent metaphor with a message for leaders: People and vision matter! If you want to generate greater commitment, initiative and strategic advantage the insights in *Exiting OZ* layout the "yellow brick road"… a great read."

Keith Thurgood
President and CEO
Overseas Military Sales Corporation

"In order to thrive, every leader can be successful when they make a promise to themselves to read and implement the wisdom in *Exiting OZ*."

Bill Bartmann
National Entrepreneur Of The Year

"*Exiting OZ* explains the inner thought process of millennials to any organization that intends to recruit, retain, and motivate top graduates. *Exiting OZ* also provides young professionals and graduating students a way to articulate their career vision clearly and avoid burnout in a "heartless, soulless, or mindless environment."

Sarah J. Shook
Undergraduate Student Body President
Minnesota Student Association

"It has become increasingly clear that a Command and Control leadership approach from a select few at the top of an organization is ineffective at managing change and strategically positioning an organization to successfully compete in a shifting and complex environment. Dr. Buffington et al, give us a model through an American archetype, i.e., *The Wizard of Oz*, to understand the traditional model of leadership and why this is not effective in the present environment.

An effective response to an environment where the future is not predictable requires a workforce that embraces the emergence of solutions to problems not yet understood or even seen. As the authors point out, Generation X and the Millennial workforce have come of age in an era of unpredictable change, rapid emergence of new technologies, and transparency whether one wants it or not.

The heroes of this generation are those able to see the patterns in the world around them and create solutions to problems we didn't know we had. Leaders in such a time must have the ability to create organizational environments where autonomy, mastery, and excitement are the common experience. The authors offer core principles through the OZ metaphor necessary to create a workforce where leadership exists at all levels and management is everyone's responsibility. Creating such a healthy environment is the essence of what Dr. Buffington et al are offering as a solution to the complexity organizations face in the present and future world."

Dr. Kevin C. Seymour, CEO
Center for Personal & Family Counseling,

Exiting OZ

By

Sherry Buffington, PhD

with

Gina Morgan

Julie Overholt

Glen Earl, PhD

Cover Design

by

Randall Reiserer and Ron Morgan

First Edition

Copyright © 2011 Sherry Buffington

Contributing Authors:
      Gina E. Morgan
      Julie Overholt
      Glen B. Earl

Cover Illustration by Randall Reiserer

Editor: Gina E. Morgan

Printed in the United States of America, Canada, and the United Kingdom

ISBN: : 978-0-9708926-3-8

QuinStar Publishing - Dallas, Texas

Acknowledgements

This book was written with the help of some very special people; my contributing authors, Gina Morgan, Julie Overholt and Glen Earl, cover designers Randall Reiserer and Ron Morgan, typesetter, Margie Baxley and my biggest supporter and cheerleader, my husband, George.

My three contributing authors are exceptional coaches and trainers with years of experience and unique talents that brought many valuable contributions to this book.

Gina Morgan is my business partner of 24 years and a co-developer of the *CORE Multidimensional Awareness Profile* (CORE MAP) and the *CORE Personal effectiveness Profile* (CORE PEP), two powerful tools for putting people in the right seats and developing them to their highest potential.

Gina is an expert on personal and interpersonal effectiveness and a trusted advisor to many high level executives. Gina has also been *my* trusted advisor for nearly thirty years. She is also my daughter so I have had the privilege of knowing her all her life and watching her develop into the amazing woman she is today. Her intelligence, deep wisdom and unwavering integrity has been a source of inspiration since she was a young girl and my appreciation of her continues to grow with every passing day.

That deep appreciation is something Gina engenders in her clients too. She doesn't just have clients, she has raving fans who are a continual testament to her skills, talents and perpetual willingness to go the extra mile. I am ever in awe of her unwavering dedication to excellence and her ability to not only produce it herself but to keep inspiring it in others.

I met Julie Overholt through the Dallas chapter of the International Coach Federation (ICF-NT) several years ago and was immediately impressed by her professionalism and intelligence. She was the president elect of ICF-NT the year I met her and I served on her board the year of her presidency. The progress the organization experienced in that year was beyond impressive, as were her exceptional leadership skills.

She inspired greatness in her board members and in the general membership while managing to remain humble and approachable throughout. Julie is an executive coach with more than two decades of experience. She is a talented advisor to leaders from mid-level managers to high-level executives as well as an able leader in her own right. Julie is an excellent model of leading authentically from both the intellect and the heart.

I met Glen Earl in 2008 when he registered for CORE facilitator training. His energy and enthusiasm made him a standout in the class he was a part of and he continued to apply himself long after the class concluded. As a fellow doctor of psychology, we had a lot in common from the outset. His enthusiasm for the CORE system added to that commonality as did the fact that Glen is an organizational psychologist and has spent many years in organizations observing the same things Gina and I have observed over the years.

As we discussed the challenges we saw emerging for organizations bent on doing business as usual, it soon became apparent that Glen's body of knowledge and area of expertise was a compliment to ours and we began to collaborate.

The insights and energy these three have brought to this endeavor have been immensely helpful in getting this book completed and I am deeply grateful for their contributions.

Gina, Julie and Glen I give you my heartfelt thanks for your contributions to this book and for your dedication and continued support.

I would also like to extend a big thank you to Randall Reiserer, the talented artist that created the illustration on the cover of this book. Thank you for taking my vision and turning it into a visual masterpiece!

Also, a big thank you to Ron Morgan, the talented and dedicated artist who completed the design work and layout for the book cover, and to Margie Baxley for typesetting the book and placing the illustrations throughout.

And last, but certainly not least, I want to acknowledge and thank my husband, George, for the patience, support and encouragement he gives so generously.

I appreciate each of you more than words can say.

Contents

Introduction
The New Reality

There is a storm brewing; a big one. One that is changing the face of the planet and every organization on it, from giant corporations to governments, to non-profit, academic, and even religious institutions —perhaps forever. You can't avoid it, but you can be prepared so when the storm hits full force, you can join the masses as they *exit* the land of OZ.

Why Exit OZ?

OZ as presented here is not the pretty, Technicolor place depicted in the MGM movie, *The Wizard of Oz*. Quite the contrary. This OZ is an ever growing nightmare that millions of people are determined to escape, and with good cause.

OZ is acronym for *Organizational Zeal*. It is the idea that an organization and its needs are more important than the people who keep it running. This has always been a mindless, heartless and soulless idea designed to keep ordinary people powerless, and self-proclaimed Wizards in control and amassing wealth. Until recently, it worked. It is not working now. In fact, in today's world, it is a predictable formula for failure.

Where people once endured OZ in the name of survival, the two newest generations, Generation X and Millennials, are creating a tornado-like backlash that is forcing organizations the world over to rethink the way they operate. Organizations that refuse to adjust will ultimately disappear and that will actually be a good thing because OZ is a demoralizing place. It drains energy, destroys initiative, engagement and trust, diminishes productivity and profits, and worst of all, robs the world of humanity and human potential.

The OZ mindset has always had a negative effect on the masses, but where previous generations endured it, today's generations actively reject it. Where previous generations only lost trust in particular organizations, today's generations distrust large organizations in general, and this overall lack of trust is driving a strong trend toward independence, entrepreneurship and a steady exodus from all kinds of OZ organizations.

This book is about that exodus, what is driving it and what organizations must do to survive and even thrive in the world that is emerging. On the surface, this book may appear rather whimsical. Don't let the title, allegories and fun illustrations fool you. This is a serious book about a very serious and growing problem. A problem that if not effectively handled in the next ten to twelve years may mean the end of long established organizations.

Many once great organizations have already followed the OZ formula to their great detriment, and many others to their demise. To date only a few organizations have successfully escaped the lure of OZ. But, make no mistake, for organizations to survive into the future, escape they must. Continuing down the same path that organizations have traveled since the industrial revolution, hoping that things will someday return to the way they once were, is a recipe for disaster. Organizations are discovering this as they struggle to meet new challenges relying on old "tried and true" methods that are just not working with the new generations.

Meet Dorothy

We begin the journey with a modern day "Dorothy", a young woman who recently graduated from a top university with honors. As you follow her and her generation through the land of OZ, you will understand why business as usual is not working anymore, and why it is unlikely to ever work again.

Throughout her school years, Dorothy was a star pupil. Even when she became a bit disillusioned by the top-rated, but staid and rather colorless university she attended, she "endured" the process to get her degree. Though much of what was required seemed pointless, she applied herself diligently believing her hard work would pay off once she graduated. She imagined a bright future and hoped that her dedication would lead to the unlimited possibilities of the dream job she imagined.

Dorothy graduated at the top of her class. She was clearly talented and intelligent so had no trouble landing a job with a top corporation right out of college. Initially, the new job and the independence it afforded her transformed her life to one of interest and excitement. It was a life full of color—Technicolor.

Dorothy entered this new world enthused and ready to give the company her best. She was excited about the opportunity to learn and be a productive member of the company team. But, for Dorothy and a growing number of people like her, the excitement was short lived.

Dorothy's employer didn't think it necessary to take the time to provide training. Company leaders took the position that employees should come in the door prepared to hit the ground running. Dorothy was told she would "figure it out" as she went. Her training consisted of "orientation", a quick scan of the company's procedures manual, a few basic instructions from her immediate supervisor, and a list of company rules.

Dorothy read through the manual and familiarized herself with the rules so she could meet expectations. She threw herself into the job and followed the rules and procedures determined to be as exemplary an employee as she had been a student. But it quickly became clear that things were not as they should be in this organization.

Management regularly preached teamwork yet avoided any kind of collaboration. People were treated inconsistently. Those with new or different ideas were routinely ignored or rejected and whenever something went wrong management was quick to point accusatory fingers at the employees. Organizational rules were rigid and many made no sense to Dorothy.

"I could have easily done my job in 3-5 hours," Dorothy reported, "but I had to stay there 8 hours a day, and sometimes longer, waiting for others to get me what I needed or waiting for the clock to run out. If the managers had been more organized, and less controlling, I really believe we could all have been far more productive and the company a lot more profitable. But the managers would not listen to the ideas or suggestions of their employees. They routinely discounted our ideas and treated us like we were total idiots. They were especially dismissive of new employees, which was very disheartening. Just because I hadn't been with a company 10 years doesn't mean I couldn't take pride in it, or do a good job, or have valid ideas. I want to be proud of the company I work for, but this company gave me very few reasons to be. A little trust would have gone a long way to motivate me and many of the others who were just as disillusioned as I was. I wasn't asking for the moon. All I wanted was respect and reasonable consideration."

Not surprisingly, Dorothy was soon looking for another place to call home. Her story is an all too common one. It's a story that gets repeated over and over again thousands of times a day in organizations all across the nation. High achievers show up willing to give their all only to have their enthusiasm dashed by the very company they seek to serve.

As organizational consultants, coaches and trainers, we frequently hear stories that make Dorothy's experience seem trivial. But this kind of experience is not trivial to Dorothy or to the tens of thousands of workers that regularly exit the corporate world in search of something better. Neither is it trivial to the organizations trying to stem that exodus.

The New Workforce

For young people just entering the workplace, landing that first job with a major corporation can be one of the most exciting days of their life—an "over the rainbow" experience—but because today's generations show up with different values and expectations than any generations before them, the initial enthusiasm quickly turns to disillusionment in typical organizations, and their usual response is to start looking for an exit.

Previous generations were willing to hang in there, even when the company's policies, positions and performance failed to consider their needs. They believed that enduring a less than ideal work environment was a necessary evil for achieving their personal and professional goals so they stayed and toughed it out.

That is not true of today's generations. Generation X and especially Millennials have observed the dissatisfaction such an approach created for their parents and grandparents, and they are not about to go down that same path. They know what they want from the workplace and they have no problem moving from one organization to another until they find one that meets their needs or until they are in a position to start their own company.

This new defiance of the work world is creating all kinds of problems for many of the old, well established organizations because they are still using those "tried and true" techniques that worked back when the organization was created. The problem is, they were created during the industrial revolution and peopled by traditional workers. We live in a whole new world now. What worked even ten years ago does not work today and will not work again in the foreseeable future.

Until organizations wake up to this new reality, they will continue to experience disengaged, "problem" employees in greater and greater numbers. They will continue to see productivity and profits slide and, unless they make some major changes, will continue to lose ground until they cease to be viable in the global marketplace.

Knowledge Workers

With today's global reach, the rapid pace and the shift to the information/technology age, the value of an organization increasingly depends upon the knowledge, dedication, and engagement of the workforce. Until recently skills in the form of physical performance drove profits and, as long as that was true, managing performance by the book was possible.

When success can be measured by the number of units a person produces, it is easy to see whether employees are applying themselves and relatively easy to enforce and/or find ways to increase that activity. But the mental application necessary for success in the information/technology age is a whole different story. Mental activity is not so easy to see, measure or enforce—and today's employees know it. Having fully engaged employees has never been more critical than it is today, and never more of a challenge for organizations as they now exist.

Today few industries can survive just having able bodied employees performing repetitive tasks. If an organization is to survive today, and certainly if it is to thrive, it must have people with specialized knowledge and skills who are *fully engaged* in their work. A body with a disengaged brain can still pull parts off an assembly line or pop rivets, but it cannot gather or properly disseminate important information or perform precision technical and problem-solving tasks.

Most organizations in the United States have not effectively made the critical transition from managing laborers to leading knowledge workers. This is partly because large organizations move slowly and are slow to change. But change they *must* because the old management models are not working well for knowledge workers in general and are not working *at all* for today's younger generations.

Failure to address the new paradigm has led to the demise of many organizations over the years. Braniff, Comp USA, Enron, Montgomery Ward, TWA, Western Auto, WorldCom and Zenith are all examples of organizations that failed primarily because they failed to adjust to a changing marketplace and to address the changing needs of their employees and customers.

It is this same myopic focus on the bottom line and blindness to the human element that keeps so many organizations scrambling to keep up and that compromises the ability of many organizations to compete effectively in the global marketplace.

Stuck in an Illusion

OZ organizations are stuck in an illusion. They still think their top leaders can run the show from behind a curtain of secrecy and can command and control their way to healthy profits. Every decision made and every action taken by OZ corporations is directly or indirectly focused on the bottom line. The leaders of these organizations adamantly assert that profit is why they are in business. "After all", they argue, "the only reason anyone goes into business is to make a profit."

Not so. Profit is certainly a reason, but not the only reason. To remain in business it is necessary to generate profits and that must always be a part of the equation. But profit is not what drives successful organizations. *Good people* drive successful organizations. *People* create the solutions that drive profits. *People* make sure systems are functioning properly. *People* make the products and services companies produce. *People* buy the products and services companies produce. *People* are the foundation of every successful organization and, for those whose products and services are intended for people, *people* are the primary reason for their existence.

OZ organizations tend to have a long running love affair with organizational structure; processes, policies, procedures, rules, regulations and perfunctory reviews. They believe rules should define people rather than people defining the rules. This is a hazardous approach with the new generations.

Many OZ organizations give lip service to a "people-centered" approach because that language is in vogue right now and they think it makes them look good, but lip service is about as far as it generally goes. Ultimately, OZ organizations are bottom-line focused and few imagine that it is about anything else.

There is no question that profits are important and even essential to an organization, but the idea that profits are *more important* than, or even possible, without people is delusional and ultimately damaging to everyone in the organization. Even those who think they are gaining something in such an environment are in fact losing, and losing big.

Organizational Zeal is the number one cause of low morale, conflict, poor employee performance, high turnover, low productivity, and lost profits in organizations of all kinds—and as everyone knows, organizations cannot exist long without profits. But to keep profits healthy the focus cannot be on profits, it must be on what generates them and that, of course, is *people.*

Theory X in OZ

In his book, *The Human Side of Enterprise*, Douglas McGregor presented his theories of workforce motivation, which he coined Theory X and Theory Y.

Theory X takes the position that people do not like to work or take responsibility and are motivated solely by money and security. Therefore they must be managed by constant supervision, tight controls and the strategic use of force and threats.

Theory Y takes the position that people enjoy work and that they are willing to put forth the required physical and mental energy. This theory holds that employees find a sense of satisfaction in the work they do. Therefore, employees require few organizational controls and minimal supervision, since motivated employees engage in self-control. They respond well to positive rewards such as recognition and empowerment, and gain intrinsic rewards for doing a "good job."

The reality is that a truly effective workplace is one that has created a very healthy balance between both of these styles. What this healthy balance looks like will become apparent as you travel through and beyond the land of OZ.

There is an abundance of "turnaround experts" who continue to teach Theory X management techniques and a plethora of OZ organizations all too willing to run down that gilded path. OZ consultants, like OZ managers, pride themselves on being tough and ruthless and they continue to preach that profits are all that matter, which is music to the ears of OZ leaders (and we use this term loosely since people focused on profits are in no way true leaders).

A classic example of the blind leading the blind is a book called *Profits Aren't Everything, They're the Only Thing*, written by Harvard Business School graduate George Cloutier, who proudly asserts that "There is a large need at all levels—whether it's the government, large corporations or small businesses—for a more tough-minded, tough-love, ruthless attitude for getting profits and the mission accomplished" (Cloutier 2009).

Sounds like going into battle, doesn't it? And that's exactly the approach OZ organizations take. They view their employees, not as prized assets, but as the enemy to be conquered.

OZ organizations flock to "experts" that hold a bottom line philosophy believing that these ruthless tactics can actually do more than temporarily stem their rapidly diminishing returns and stave off their eventual demise.

Cloutier proudly positions himself as a "sensitive tyrant" which he explains means that he stays sensitive to what is going on around him by requiring reports from every department every day. He has taken his "get tougher" message and methods into more than 2,500 organizations since 1986. We can assume that he and his team were invited into all these organizations because each of the organizations still hold to the old OZ Theory X belief that you only get the best from people when it is coerced out of them. The problem with this approach is that it doesn't work anymore and won't again in our lifetimes. OZ consultants are comforting to OZ leaders because they reinforce their delusions and give them a false sense of security. The problem is that they are all about to go over a cliff together and no one is able to see it.

Sorry OZites, the Truth is Going to Hurt

This book is not for organizations that hang their hopes on the "get tougher" philosophies. It is not about getting tougher. It is about getting smarter, wiser and more accurately attuned to the realities of today's changing world. It is about backing up and taking a clear-eyed view of what really works and what doesn't in the world we have created and making new choices to thrive in it.

It takes vision, wisdom, heart and courage to step away from the old, outdated practices and venture into new, mostly uncharted territory— and it takes humility—something OZ leaders find very disdainful.

OZ leaders will hate this book. Most will not see any reason to read it because they think they already have all the answers they need. If they did read it, this is about as far as they would get because the idea that what they are doing is not working and will never work again is too scary. The suggestion that to be effective today will require them to drastically change the way they lead will not be welcome or even acceptable news to the typical OZ leader. It's much easier to argue the point than make the changes, but change they must if they are to survive because not only are the new generations refusing to work for OZ organizations, increasingly they are also refusing to *buy* from them.

For Progressive Leaders

This book is for leaders whose organization adopted the old corporate model because it was the one most readily available and most often taught in the old, staid institutions. It is for leaders that have seen and acknowledged that this model no longer works and who are looking for something that *will*. It is for leaders who genuinely want to lead better; who are struggling to understand why all the things they are trying in an effort to attract and retain top performers and make a healthy profit continue to fall short.

This book is for progressive leaders who want to grow healthy, viable organizations and who understand that the path to that end is filled with fully engaged, highly productive people performing at peak levels—leaders who are willing to set aside preconceived notions and try something radically new and different. It is for leaders that are willing to step boldly into the twenty-first century and learn to lead the people of today in the way they need to be led.

If you are a progressive leader, know that there *is* a way to get your organization to where you want it to go and it may be a lot easier than you now imagine.

As you journey with us through the land of OZ you may recognize some unhealthy habits you have adopted from old school institutions and corporations, and from the "experts" who advise them. By recognizing unproductive behaviors you will have the opportunity to replace them with healthier alternatives and begin getting the exceptional outcomes you envision. In reality, the new leadership model is much easier and much more effective than the old one. It takes a lot of pressure off of leaders by distributing responsibility more evenly among the entire employee population. Under this model leaders do less and employees do more—and *love* it!

For OZ Dissidents

This book is also for people who are currently employed in OZ organizations and are, predictably, dissatisfied and searching for a workplace to call home. You can save yourself many years of wasted time and a world of grief by recognizing and avoiding organizations stuck in the land of OZ. This book will help you do that. If discovering ways to ensure a more purposeful work life and a more profitable future is your goal, the journey through OZ will be one journey you will be glad you took.

> "Toto, I've a feeling we're not in Kansas anymore…
> We MUST be over the rainbow!"
>
> Dorothy - From *The Wizard of Oz*

CHAPTER ONE
"I Don't Think We're in Kansas Anymore Toto"

From the outside, many OZ organizations look safe and appealing. Possibilities and opportunities seem to abound. But, all is not as it appears in the land of OZ.

In OZ, actually getting your hands on the opportunities you imagine are there can be a very long journey fraught with scary encounters and difficult challenges. As long as you stay true to the OZ agenda, you might do okay, but try to innovate or do something different; or start thinking of yourself or your family rather than the organization's agenda and you will soon find yourself quaking before the great and powerful Wizard.

In "Kansas" that is, on your own home turf, the rules are well known. You know what you can and cannot do. You know what will get you in trouble and what will result in a reward.

In OZ the rules you have learned at home do not apply. OZ operates under its own rules, which may or may not be conveyed to you. And it's up to you to figure out how to navigate them. If you do it poorly, forget about getting what you came for.

If you do it well—you *might* get the reward you are after—but then again you might not. It depends on the mood and current mindset of the Wizard, or perhaps on what the Wizard has decided you want or need.

In OZ you are not consulted so what you want is not really known. The Wizard decides. You either like what is provided or you don't, but the choice is not yours. You must just take what is given and be grateful—or leave.

Figuring out how to navigate an OZ organization is not unlike Dorothy's journey through the storied Land of Oz. It can be confusing, frustrating and even frightening. There are lots of ambiguities which almost all employees find frustrating and stress inducing. Yet, different generations have handled the frustrations and ambiguities very differently.

The Exodus

It is the way the newer generations are reacting to OZ organizations that has resulted in the mass exodus organizations have seen in recent years. If this trend is not adequately addressed and stemmed, corporations will continue to lose the best and brightest employees which will seriously compromise the viability of some of America's longest established corporations in the next few years.

The high cost of bureaucratic leadership became quite obvious in 2009 when the banking and auto manufacturing industries rushed to the government for bailout funds and then used large portions of those funds to reward themselves for the debacle they had created.

The same destructive management practices are occurring in OZ organizations across the nation and in the government itself, and surface measures will not fix the problem. Unless some foundational changes are made, and soon, we will all suffer the consequences to a far greater degree than we now do, and perhaps than we now even imagine.

A new workforce with a whole new mindset and a whole new approach to life and work has emerged, and their unwillingness to follow OZ rules will have far reaching consequences. The effect of this new approach has already begun to be felt in America's corporations, but they haven't seen anything yet.

Unlike the Traditional and Baby Boom generations which learned to navigate the hierarchical command and control leadership and deal with the wide chasm that separated top management from the workforce, the new workforce made up of Generation X and Millennials has other ideas, other ideals and completely different beliefs.

The workers that organizations across the country are beginning to inherit are not quite so willing to go down that road. Their unwillingness is, in part, why there is an ever growing tension in today's workplaces and an ever growing insecurity on the part of corporate leaders around finding and keeping high performers.

Attracting and retaining high performance employees has become a primary concern as Baby Boomers begin to retire and younger generations continue to reject the corporate model. And the way most organizations are going about addressing this problem is a formula for disaster.

Studies conducted by Michigan State University indicate that "about two million people voluntarily quit their jobs in the United States every month—and most of these people will try again to look for new jobs and satisfying careers" (Chao and Gardner 2007).

Even when OZ organizations manage to attract talented workers they don't tend to keep them for long, for reasons that will become all too obvious as you continue the journey through the land of OZ.

Old Rules in a New World Do Not Compute

Although the marketplace has changed, customers have changed and certainly the workforce has changed, many organizations are stuck in the past, still trying to run the company as though the old traditional work ethic still existed and command and control management still worked.

Old school leaders complain loudly about the lack of work ethic and the poor attitudes of today's generations. They complain that the younger generations want too much and that their wants are unrealistic and unreasonable.

A classic lament from unenlightened leaders is that newer generations come in the door wanting to be the vice president and don't want to pay their dues to get there. They complain that the younger workers don't follow rules the way traditional workers did and are not loyal.

Hearing these laments over and over again is what started me searching for answers as to why this dynamic existed. More than a dozen years of research and conferring with other consultants, coaches, trainers and organizational psychologists, such as my contributing authors, led me to see that, while the complaints certainly had some basis in fact, there was a lot more to it than most assumed.

What I discovered is that the current organizational structure, environment and leadership styles that pervade most large organizations drive the observed behaviors of today's workforce as much as their mindset and values. The two are like oil and water, and it is unlikely that they will ever mix well.

Different Rules

The emerging workforce plays by different rules to be sure. This is the new reality and one today's leaders must successfully deal with if they want to survive and thrive. Everyone seems to know this except OZ leaders.

In the wildly popular book *The 4-Hour Work Week,* Gen X author, Tim Ferris lays out a plan for building a successful one-person business and encourages people to abandon the insanity of the rat race and build their own personal empire.

Another recent book, *Crush It! Why Now is the Time to Cash in on Your Passions* by Gen Xer Gary Vaynerchuk, pushes the message out even farther. He says, "There is no excuse for anyone living in the United States or anywhere else right now to slog through his or her entire life working at jobs they hate, or even jobs they simply don't love, in the name of a paycheck or a sense of responsibility. The internet makes it possible for anyone to be 100 percent true to themselves and make serious cash by turning what they love most into their personal brand. There no longer has to be a difference between who you are and what you do" (Vaynerchuk 2009).

Corporate executives are not likely reading these books, but they should be. They can learn something about the workforce they are about to inherit. Even the established business guru, Michael Gerber, in his most recent book *The Most Successful Small Business in the World,* observes that we are "in the age of the new entrepreneur," an age "where individuals rule." And where individuals rule, the games OZ corporations play don't fly.

Through interviewing thousands of young workers, I have found that Generation X and Millennials don't really come in the door of an organization expecting a position of power—at least not in the way many leaders think.

They don't walk in the door expecting to become the vice president, but they *do* come in expecting a high degree of consideration and inclusion. They *do* want to be seen as individuals with value and contributions to make, and they do want the opportunity to make those contributions. They also want to know what is going on in the company they work for and how they fit into the big picture. They aren't necessarily pushing for positional power, but they do want, and insist upon, *personal* power.

Their insistence on being considered and informed is often misinterpreted as arrogance and generalized to "they think they ought to be the president" assumptions, but that is not where most of them are coming from. Because the newer generations are not playing by OZ rules they can appear to lack commitment and dedication. Because they know what they want and are willing to go after it even if it means they must sacrifice something, they can appear unrealistic and unreasonable, at least to those accustomed to the "pay your dues" rules.

In the right environment, however, these young people have proven to be bright, technically savvy, dedicated, and fiercely loyal to their employers.

Just ask Google or Intuit or one of the other progressive companies that employ them.

In OZ organizations, people who dare come in the door with their own goals and visions; who try to change the status quo and forge new ways of doing business, even if they are potentially better ways, are bound to be seen by OZites as unrealistic, undisciplined, lacking a work ethic and just generally hard to manage.

The reality is that the new generations *are* hard to manage by the old rules. In fact, managing them by the old rules is next to impossible! The big question is not whether today's workers will ever follow the old rules (they won't), but why managers and leaders keep trying to operate within the old rules when doing so is predictably a losing battle.

If It Isn't Working, Try Something Else

The tactics OZ organizations take in an effort to increase compliance and get better results are clearly not working. But rather than adjust, some organizations simply impose stricter rules, crack the whip louder or try to hire, fire and rehire their way to compliance.

Others go searching for new ways to apply the old rules believing they are being innovative and doing everything possible to improve performance. Then, as each effort fails, managers get more and more frustrated, and most are at a complete loss as to what to try next.

As the situation worsens, many organizations become willing to try almost anything—as long as it fits into the established structure. When their efforts fail and they can't figure out what to do next, the old school managers typically fall back on the assumption that the younger generations just don't get it and continue to blame them.

The problem is, OZ leaders are pointing fingers in the wrong direction. They would be better served by looking at the rules, regulations, management practices, procedures, expectations and assumptions of the organization.

Disconnected from Reality

Through many years of research and working with leaders and employees across many industries in hundreds of organizations, what we frequently discover is that management, while greatly concerned about employee performance, is disconnected from the reality of employee needs.

The government requirement that students and other applicants have good credit before they can get a federal job is a classic example. A smarter approach would be to hire people and give those whose credit has suffered from their being unemployed a year to improve their credit score and then provide classes to teach them how to do that. I suspect their problems with a "shrinking eligible pool" would quickly shrink if they did that one small thing.

An experience I had in 1996 makes this point quite well too. Because I always guarantee results, before I will accept any job I make it a point to fully understand the problem, formulate a specific plan for solving it and get the cooperation of leaders in implementing the plan. If any one of these is missing, I do not proceed.

In this instance, I was called into a large organization which, two years earlier, had implemented a program designed to unify employees (which presumably included management). "The power of one" was upper management's mantra. The problem was that, instead of improving morale, teamwork and productivity, things had steadily gotten worse. Employees were sullen and cranky, and petty wars were raging everywhere.

The first thing I did was question employees in confidential interviews and really listen to what they had to say. Essentially, what they told me was that they had been collectively wounded by the uncaring attitudes and lack of concern they regularly detected in management, especially at the top three levels.

Prior to the implementation of the infamous program, many of the employees had voiced their concerns about the employee/leadership gap and management's answer had been this "joke of a program". As far as the employees were concerned, the "power of one" was conferred on just one person; the guy at the top.

Almost every employee I interviewed commented that nothing had changed in the company after the installation of the expensive program except that they (the employees) were now supposed to pretend that everything was all better.

The company had spent almost a million dollars on this program and the managers were always quick to point this out. With each complaint or suggestion for improvement, employees were reminded of the large investment the company had made "for the employees' sake" and told that they should be more grateful.

But they were *not* grateful. They were *furious*! And their furor is what drove their attitudes and behaviors on the job. The employees well knew that their productivity had decreased and their behaviors worsened. They didn't care! They wanted to be seen, heard and acknowledged in a genuine way, and they had no intention of making any improvements until they were.

Unfortunately for this company and its employees, the guy at the top, the self-proclaimed Wizard, was too insecure, self-absorbed and separated from the reality of the workplace to consider that his approach might be the problem. He had carefully surrounded himself with people who would agree with him and bow to his whims, so the two tiers of management below him just blindly followed his lead. The top guy refused to hear and acknowledge what the employees were trying so desperately to convey in both words and deeds, or to make the requested changes, and his entourage kept silent.

In spite of the overwhelming evidence that there was a leadership problem, upper management insisted that the real problem was the employees and that the answer to "insubordinate behavior" was to tighten controls, eliminate incentives, more strictly enforce the rules, and train the employees to perform better. Any suggestions coming from the ranks and directed toward the generals were summarily dismissed.

Their response to my recommendations was pretty much the same as it had been to employee suggestions. They side-stepped the recommendations for changes in leadership practices and requested that I "just fix the employees".

Surface change is not my style. I consider it a terrible waste of resources, so to stay in integrity with my values I opted not to continue working with the company. Even if the managers had agreed to waive my guarantee, which I require when I don't get full cooperation, I knew trying to "fix" the employees was not the answer. To proceed as requested would have just increased the frustration of the employees and been a waste of the company's time and money. I declined the job.

Ultimately and predictably, the brightest, most employable people continued to leave the company in a steady stream to work elsewhere. The job turnover rate in this organization continued to be extremely high and productivity appallingly low. About two years after my encounter with this organization, it was in such deep trouble that it ended up being sold to a competitor at bargain basement rates.

The problems continued to exist in this company to its demise because a vicious cycle had developed and only healthy intervention at the top could have stopped it. Healthy intervention rarely occurs, however, until the ineffective leader retires and is replaced with a good leader or until the pain becomes so unbearable and the losses so great that stakeholders decide to intervene.

The problem with this company was that it was a publicly traded utility with thousands of stockholders, most of whom were as disconnected as management, and the cost of management blunders could just be passed on to their customers—to a point. Deregulation became the death knell for this organization. Once customers had other choices the company quickly and predictably began losing ground.

Passing the Buck

Passing the buck, as well as the cost of blunders, on to customers is a typical OZ response. Not all organizations can get by with it, but far too many can and do. That too is changing. Today's consumers are far more informed and savvy. They can go to the internet and research companies worldwide. They can buy globally as well as locally and nationally. They know they have choices and more and more of them are exercising that freedom. Unless an organization has a complete monopoly, which is rare these days, the choice to pass the cost of ineffective management on to consumers, rather than fix the problem and stay competitive, is a choice for failure.

Sending jobs overseas to reduce costs is another practice that is about to have serious repercussions because today's savvy buyers can research the companies they buy from, and many are choosing to do just that. And Generation X and especially Millennials are looking further into the future and at a broader picture than just the quality or cost of a product. They are looking at how fair and responsible the practices of the companies they choose to buy from are. And more and more they are rejecting organizations that are too focused on the bottom line to care about the affect of their actions on the people in their community.

Sending jobs overseas may cut costs, but it will also cut sales as the new, more community-minded generations become the majority in the customer pool.

The only way to succeed in a transparent world filled with enlightened workers and conscientious consumers is to get connected—*really* connected—and get real. Organizations must learn to serve, both their employees and their customers. Loyalty begats loyalty. It cannot be demanded and it cannot be faked.

CHAPTER TWO
The Munchkins Emerge

Until the Baby Boom generation, workers generally accepted the role of little people. They showed up to work every day, put in long hours, followed the rules, and did whatever it took to keep the company running smoothly. They kept as low a profile as was necessary to prevent upsetting the Wizard, and most would never have dreamed of questioning the big man's directives.

Then a few enlightened souls appeared among the traditional workers and began questioning the wisdom of remaining silent. They formed unions that gave them a voice and they began teaching their children, the Baby Boomers, to look at leadership in a different light.

With the encouragement of the enlightened Traditionalists, the "little people" slowly and cautiously began to emerge. Once they stepped out of the shadows and realized the strength of their collective voices, they slowly began claiming their own power and teaching their children to do the same.

Like the house that destroyed the Wicked Witch of the East, labor unions stepped up and squashed the idea of complete control and tyranny that had been such a part of early command and control leadership. Although there were improvements, the authoritarian management style was well entrenched and the tyranny did not end. Still, the little people were empowered to emerge from the shadows and they did so in greater and greater numbers.

A New Attitude

The courage of the people in stepping from the shadows and into the light didn't change the thinking or actions of OZ leaders much, but it changed the thinking and attitudes of the employees and led to a new way of thinking for future generations.

Even though Baby Boomers were often referred to as the "me" generation by those seeking to control them, the Boomers knew that self-consideration was not a bad thing so they refused to allow that unflattering moniker to alter their awareness of themselves or undermine their determination to find their own version of fulfillment.

Yet, as a whole, the Baby Boom generation was much like the unaware, unevolved Dorothy who set out on the yellow brick road in search of a way home. The Boomers didn't have the answers yet and were still somewhat afraid to step out too far, but they were emboldened to at least take the journey and approach the Great OZ to ask for what they wanted.

Though Baby Boomers were willing to take new risks and go after what they wanted, they had not yet come to realize that the Wizard didn't have the power or inclination to give them what they were working so hard to earn. This generation continued to believe in and serve their leader and to allow him to remain sequestered away in his castle—within limits.

Let an OZ leader prove unworthy of their trust and the Boomers were quick to expose them, then turn away and go looking for another company to call home—a practice that was not lost on their children.

What Baby Boomers were willing to consider "home" just needed to be reasonably comfortable. To their more enlightened children that is not the case. Generation X was given a voice and choices by their Boomer parents, so this new generation entered the workforce with a whole new perspective on what the work world should be like. To Generation X just having a reasonably comfortable environment is not enough. To them "home" is far more than that.

For Generation X and the most recent generation, Millennials, "home" is a company that is considerate of their individual needs; not just when consideration is convenient, but all the time. They want a place that values them as human beings and treats them like a member of a caring family. They want both comfort and respect. They want to be kept informed. They want to do meaningful work for a worthwhile cause. And they insist that the company they stay with provide more than just a paycheck. They need a personally satisfying reason to be there.

Sadly, the organizations that get it and are taking steps to meet the new reality are still few and far between, which is why today's workforce changes jobs so frequently.

According to an article in Forbes Magazine "today a typical American holds more than eight different jobs between the ages of 18 and 32 alone. Recent research shows that 85% of American workers expect to be employed by a new company within 12 months" (Kenny 2007). What this means is that they leave one company actively looking for another.

Because traditionalists have mostly retired and left the workforce, the traditional work ethic has left with them. Gone are the days of staying with one company for thirty years and being content to silently and dutifully follow the rules until it's time to retire and collect the gold watch.

It isn't that today's workers are fickle and just want new scenery, as many OZ leaders assert. Most of the people I have interviewed, both young and more mature, tell me they would love to find a company in which they could feel at home and where they could stay until they were ready to retire. Most people hate the idea of continual job hunting, but find the idea of oppression even more distasteful. Employees are not jumping ship because they are bored with the scenery. They are jumping in search of the right fit. As one Millennial put it, "I would love to stay with one organization until I retire, but I am not willing to give up my ideals and identity to do that."

The newer generations strongly desire the American dream promise of opportunity and continual growth; of fairness and trust and better days ahead; of a means to build a secure future, but they don't believe that the dream is alive anymore. Their hopes and dreams are not different than previous generations. What *is* different is the trust factor.

Like Generation X and Millennials, many Baby Boomers are actively looking for ways to leave OZ organizations today. The older ones are retiring and starting their own businesses and the younger ones are keeping their names in front of head hunters, knowing there is a coming labor shortage and a predicted "brain drain" as experienced workers begin to retire. This makes them very valuable assets and they are open to leveraging that fact.

2020 Vision

By the year 2020, Generation X and Millennials will make up about ninety percent of the workforce, and these generations are writing their own rules. To them the old rules seem illogical. They make no sense and are not worth following. These generations have seen behind "the curtain".

They know what's back there and they are *not* impressed. They refuse to be relegated to the role of "Munchkins", the little people who bow to the Wizard and never question his power, authority or wisdom.

Until the emergence of Generation X and Millennials, OZ organizations were better able to keep and control employees by meting out predictable raises, bonuses and promotions. As long as the "rewards" kept coming and things didn't get too bad, the Wizard was dutifully obeyed and allowed to remain hidden away in a distant castle relatively free from the direct scrutiny of the workforce.

Only those with appointed power entered that high domain, and then only to gather orders or talk about concessions the Wizard was willing to make to the unions. Ultimately, the power of the unions proved insufficient to dethrone the Wizard, but it was sufficient to raise awareness of individual rights and that was enough to forever change the dynamics of the American workplace.

OZ leaders are not happy with this fact and many prefer to ignore it, hoping it will eventually go away and things will return to "normal". What they fail to realize is that what they are experiencing today *is* normal. This is the way things are, not just in isolated pockets here and there, but everywhere.

The new reality is not like some virus that will clear up in time. Quite the contrary; it grows ever stronger as the workforce fills with more and more Gen Xers and Millennials. The reality is that organizations have about ten years to learn how to work with these new generations. Those who are ready to learn and willing to ride this new wave will discover a workforce that can perform amazing feats. Those who keep fighting the reality and fail to get it right will eventually die. That may sound harsh, but the evidence is mounting daily to validate the accuracy of this claim.

What OZ leaders are grasping for is gone and will *not* return—at least not in the foreseeable future. To survive and once again thrive in the new reality, OZ leaders must get out from behind the curtain and *get real*. It's the only way they will have anyone to lead in the future because the independent, empowered munchkins are not about to settle for anything less.

CHAPTER THREE
Follow the Yellow Brick Road

To the workforce, the Yellow Brick Road represents the path to opportunity and success. In the world of OZ, however, this path means strictly following the rules and, for OZ organizations, the rules of the road are highly structured. They are designed to ensure that everyone proceeds along the path at the organizationally prescribed pace and in whatever way the OZ leader thinks appropriate.

In OZ organizations employees are told early on that, if they just stay on the path and keep moving in the prescribed manner, they may in time get the attention of the great Wizard and gain a reward. They learn through the grapevine that the Wizard either grants or denies wishes, depending on how well those who travel the road perform. And, since the Wizard is the one that decides who gets rewarded and who does not, pleasing him becomes a primary goal.

The overly strict requirement to adhere to prescribed rules, processes and procedures with little concern for how they affect the people is what creates OZ organizations in the first place—and they span the gamut. OZ organizations are not just bureaucratic corporations, they exist in many places and wherever they exist, there is an ongoing struggle between the organization and its more enlightened people.

Staid old schools and universities struggle with new generation teachers who can see the fallacy of one-size-fits-all learning and adherence to old, outdated information. New generation teachers want to create innovative new models to meet the needs of all learning styles. Like their progressive corporate counterparts, they are not willing to deal with all the politics so the best and brightest either find a way to create an innovative department and buck the system, or they leave often opting to work for the more progressive private schools. The staid old schools are finding themselves struggling more and more with teachers who have "the audacity" to demand the kind of education they believe students need and deserve.

Dogmatic churches struggle with new generation clergy and new generation members who chafe at strict dogma and prefer to address religion in more holistic and healing ways; who prefer to approach the spiritual aspects of life from a more open-minded and inclusive perspective rather than condemning those who hold different views.

Undemocratic governments and dictatorships worldwide are finding it ever more difficult and expensive to try to keep their citizens subjected and subdued. And governments that call themselves democratic, but have become so mired in politics and getting re-elected that they have lost sight of the fact that they are there to serve the people are finding it more and more difficult to keep their self-centered agendas secret.

More and more of the world population has joined the ranks of those who resist processes, procedures and rules which they perceive as heartless, mindless and soulless. They are defecting in groves, and the trend is likely to accelerate as the new generations become the mainstream majority.

Generational studies suggest that actively involved Millennials, which are seventy million strong, will surpass the Baby Boom generation in the workplace by 2020. Remember, this is the generation that would rather keep jumping ship than be saddled with OZ rigidity.

Enlightened, Disgusted and Rewriting the Rules

We see this trend at work both inside organizations and outside as governments at every level, from local to national, struggle to balance the will of enlightened and now angry and disgusted citizens, impatient for real change, with the demands of OZ sponsored lobbyists who want to keep things the same.

To the entrepreneurially minded employee of today, the Yellow Brick Road as laid out by OZ organizations is not too appealing. To them the road to opportunity and success is much more friendly and flexible.

Today's workers believe organizational structure should serve only to guide and inform their choices as they move toward their goals; that it should in no way hinder or constrain them.

As a mere guideline, the rules of the road look much different than OZ organizations imagine. So while today's employees are flexing, and changing the rules as they go, OZ organizations are digging in their heels and insisting that people follow established rules and not stray from the road they have so carefully laid out.

The insistence upon following strict, unyielding, "my way or the highway" rules aren't working anymore, but the Wizard is too disconnected to see that. As a result, disagreements and discord between OZ leaders at every level and today's generations continue to mount. And it is the OZ leaders that will be left behind.

In the workplace, as in every other arena, this battle is likely to rage on until one side concedes. In that business organizations cannot operate without loyal, dedicated workers and today's workers refuse to give unearned loyalty and dedication, it doesn't take a rocket scientist to figure out who is going to win this battle.

A Different Story

In spite of the insistence of OZ leaders that today's workforce is uncommitted and unwilling to do the job, that is often not the reality. Our research as well as that of many organizational consultants presents a very different story. The picture that continues to emerge in studying Generation X and Millennials is that of technologically savvy people with a deep desire to contribute in real and meaningful ways. They are completely unwilling to compromise their values and neither Generation X nor Millennials see the OZ way of doing business as meaningful or in step with today's world. The majority of them are not willing to travel too far down that road and they make no excuses for that.

The impact of the resistance from the newer generations was aptly described in an article published in 2008 in Workforce Management Magazine in an interview of Libby Sartain, a former VP of HR for Southwest Airlines and Yahoo. Sartain observed that "the talent marketplace in the last two or three years has changed so dramatically that almost everything we do in HR has got to change with it." She sees the drastic changes as a natural evolution of the internet, social media, the global economy, and of Generation X and Millennials coming of age and entering the workforce as Baby Boomers are leaving.

Though most companies don't yet recognize this reality, the challenges they face in this new world are reflected in Sartain's observation that businesses can no longer just recruit for an opening and get an employee. "The company used to be in the driver's seat" she states, "where employers regularly took the position of 'Here's the job I have. Here's how much I want to pay you to do this work. Come to work for me under my terms as the employer'. That is no longer the case," she states.

We concur with Sartain's observation that the marketplace is evolving and will continue to evolve. "It is almost to the point that you have a marketplace like eBay," Sartain says, "where someone will put themselves out to bid: 'Here I am. Here's what I'm willing to do for how much money I'm willing to make. Here are my hours and my location and what I can do for you.' It's going to be the employee in the driver's seat" (Frauenheim 2008).

The employees Sartain is describing are primarily Generation X and Millennials, but even Baby Boomers have begun looking for more flexibility at work and in their lifestyles, and are making this shift. Sartain observes that this new way of doing business is especially true for top talent and core talent in certain industries, such as technology and information processing, and asserts that this trend is going to sweep the country in the very near future. Are you listening OZites?

The Group Exodus

From all we can gather, Sartain is right. In Silicon Valley employees joke that the best "techies" can change jobs without even changing their carpool because they offer themselves to new employers as a team and the entire team gets hired away from their current employer.

In Dallas recently two young Gen Xers proudly told me about their newly formed company and the great team they had in place from day one. They started out with a great team because they left a dysfunctional organization and took an entire technical department with them.

They explained that they had tried on many occasions to get the organization's leaders to improve working conditions, but had gotten nowhere. So they collectively decided they could never get their needs met in that organization and the entire department left and started their own company. Imagine the cost to the organization of losing their *entire* technical department!

An Entrepreneurial Mindset

The journey to opportunity and success looks very different today than it did when OZ built the corporate road. No doubt the road as it was built has its places of interest as well as its hazards, but the warnings issued by OZ officials to stay on the path and not stray from it are beginning to fall on deaf ears.

Today's employees are more entrepreneurially minded than any generation since America was founded. They are not content to simply follow rules laid down by someone else and stay within a defined structure that they disagree with. They want to innovate and try new things.

They look down that long road and see how very far away the Emerald City (opportunity for success) really is, and they start looking for short cuts. They will follow the road only insofar as it makes sense and looks interesting. If they find a shorter route to their goals, they have no problem leaving the road to explore other avenues.

Because attracting and retaining top talent is critical to the success of any enterprise, companies need to be aware of, and eliminate, the hazards that compel their best and most promising employees to go in search of other options.

The primary hazard is weak or misguided leadership. For some leaders, the hazard is created by short-sighted thinking. For others, it is rigidity and insistence on adhering to the "get it done and get it right" thinking that continues to dominate at the expense of employee satisfaction. For others emotional intelligence is lacking so leaders are erratic and unpredictable, and for still others it is lack of courage in making the right choices, especially when they are hard choices.

It is important to understand the various forms of hazardous leadership and how they impact the organization and its people, so we will be covering each in more depth in the following chapters.

If OZ corporations want to sustain their place in the land of opportunity and success; if they are ever to rise above the self-created fortress-turned-prison they have created, they too will need to change the way they think about the journey.

Scarecrow: I haven't got a brain... only straw.
Dorothy: How can you talk if you haven't got a brain?
Scarecrow: I don't know... But some people without brains do an awful lot of talking... don't they?
Dorothy: Yes, I guess you're right.

From *The Wizard of Oz*

CHAPTER FOUR
If I Only Had a Brain: Recognizing the Scarecrow

Meet the Scarecrow leader. In the world of OZ, the Scarecrow is the manager who has very little spine and a mostly disengaged brain. This individual falls apart too easily and even though he or she has the brains and ability to do better, this fact is rarely self-recognized or taken advantage of.

Scarecrows mindlessly follow organizational rules and, because they do, they tend to move along the organizational path relatively well as long as there are no hazards along the way. Since they fall apart easily, they typically do everything they can to avoid hazards, and just blindly following the leader is a good way to do that.

Just as the Scarecrow in the movie *The Wizard of Oz* relied heavily on Dorothy, his leader, to put him back together when he fell apart, so too do corporate Scarecrows.

A major complaint of upper level managers is how much time they spend supporting the managers in their charge who fall apart too easily under pressure. This is often an emotional intelligence deficit more than a mental deficit. It just appears to be a mental deficit because those who lack emotional intelligence also lack confidence so are reluctant to engage the brains they actually do have.

In many OZ organizations, Scarecrows get promoted to higher and higher positions in spite of the fact that their brain is largely disengaged. Whether or not they are smart or talented, they follow the rules and play the game well, and that is what OZ leaders are most interested in.

In time, some of the Scarecrows even reach high enough positions to be the ones who decide how the organization gets run—sort of. They are still following the orders of the invisible Wizard, but few people know that.

When a Scarecrow is the CEO of an OZ organization, it appears he is the one calling the shots, but this is just another illusion. Those who are watching that ever important bottom line are always the ones calling the shots in OZ organizations.

Because Scarecrows have no spine and have not fully engaged their brains, they can wreak havoc throughout an organization when they are the figurehead. And they often do. One way they do that is through the mindless implementation of the downsizing cycle.

When the Wizard; that invisible someone that stays focused on the bottom line, decides that the profits are not good enough, he calls in the Scarecrow, points to a diminishing bottom line and tells him the problem must be fixed immediately.

To comply, the brainless Scarecrow peruses the income and expense reports and notices that the greatest expense is employee salaries. Because his brain is not engaged and he can't see past the numbers, he fails to see that employees are also the company's means for generating income. He can't see that, when properly motivated and directed, the employees are the company's greatest asset—that engaged, productive employees are by far the *best* way to increase profits. He can't see that inspiring the workforce to higher performance, greater productivity and more efficient functioning is the fastest, surest and most sustainable way of increasing profits.

All the Scarecrow is looking at is the bottom line so all he can see is the cost and decides the best way to make the bottom line look better is to reduce the workforce. He sends out the news that the company has to downsize to cut costs and gives the order to start chopping heads. And the organization's slow, painful journey to destruction begins.

Most organizational consultants know that it is not possible to cost cut your way to success, but the Scarecrow never seems to get this, and the Wizard is too removed from reality to know what is happening until it is too late.

Here's how the journey to destruction typically goes:

- A percentage of employees get fired and/or laid-off, often with no consideration for what the employees do or do not contribute. All too often longevity is what determines who stays and who goes because the organization has no effective way of measuring productivity. As a result, engaged, productive employees are let go while many who have been there for a longer time, mostly because they know how to stay under the radar, remain.

- The remaining employees see that their jobs are at risk and fear that they might be next to go so they work extra hard to prove their worth.

- Fewer employees working harder generate more profits at less cost so for awhile the bottom line improves. The Wizard is happy and the Scarecrow congratulates himself for a job well done.

- Over time, however, the strain of trying to do the work of two or three people, combined with fear of being fired if profits don't meet the Wizard's expectations, begins to take its toll on the remaining employees, and they start to burn out.

- As stress mounts, the best workers (those who believe they are good enough to find a job in a better environment) quit, leaving those who are less confident about their employability and less capable of exceptional performance with an even greater burden.

- In time the best employees have left and those remaining are overloaded and burned out, so once again profits drop.

- The Wizard notices that profits aren't looking so good again and again calls in the Scarecrow. Since neither bother to think broadly enough or look far enough ahead to consider what might have gone wrong, the Scarecrow simply repeats the process and the whole cycle begins anew. Each time the cycle repeats itself, employees become more fearful, more stressed, more overworked and more unproductive.

Unless the Scarecrow finally engages his brain or is replaced by someone who already has one fully engaged, the predictable result is the eventual demise of the company. This occurs time and time again in organizations of every size.

The High Cost of Misguided Leadership

Study the failure of corporate giants such as Western Auto, Montgomery Ward, TWA, WorldCom, Braniff, Enron and Comp USA, and in every instance you will find that the demise came as a result of misguided leadership.

Let's look at Western Auto as an example. According to the history laid out in the book entitled *The Last Western Flyer: The Western Auto Century* by Dr. Jim Marchman, Western Auto Supply Company was a chain of automobile parts stores that was started in 1909. It started as a mail order business for replacement auto parts and opened its first retail store in 1921.

As automobiles became more and more common and the demand for parts increased, Western Auto grew. At its peak there were over 1,200 company-owned stores nationwide and more than 600 dealer owned (franchise) stores. They were so successful that they began reinvesting money into Western Auto brands, such as Western Flyer bicycles and Performance Radial GT tires. They acquired other companies and further expanded their product line to include things like rifles and shotguns.

When Wal-Mart appeared on the scene in the early 1960s, Western Auto tried to compete by converting all of the company-owned stores to what they called flag stores which sold only automotive parts and accessories.

With the typical myopia of OZ leaders, they strongly urged all of their stores to switch their merchandising approach and stock at least 50% automotive parts. The merchants in dealer-owned stores refused because they were typically located in small towns and their customers needed a wider range of merchandise. It was the foresight, determination and "rebelliousness" of the dealer-owned stores that kept Western Auto alive for as long as it was.

By 1987 Western Auto was floundering and they sold their interests to Sears Roebuck. Sears added Craftsman tools and DieHard batteries to the product line, but the culture never changed and the same old mistakes continued to be made. By 1997 more than a third of the company-owned stores were closed and the dealer-owned stores, those that belonged to the rebels, were what was keeping the company afloat.

Continued lack of focus and mismanagement induced Sears to sell the Western Auto division in 1997 and by 2003 it was dead. The new owners notified the rebel store owners that they would need to find other supply sources, which was no problem for many because they were already buying much of their merchandise from other sources anyway. However, they had to operate under a different name, because the parent company whose name they had proudly displayed for almost 50 years was now gone (Marchman 2008).

This story has been repeated hundreds of times over the years; thousands of times if we include the less well known companies, and still many corporations are playing the same losing game. Why? Because they live in the land of OZ and think it's a real place.

Scarecrow managers do have brains, of course, but sadly they rarely use them. Scarecrows are conflict avoidant and prefer no decision to a decision that might upset someone. They frequently defer decisions to others to avoid creating situations that may lead to disagreement. Their indecisiveness is not about what is best for the organization, but about what will help them avoid discomfort in dealing with others, especially those they view as superiors.

Recognizing Scarecrows

- Pander to superiors.

- Do whatever the Wizard says without questioning the wisdom of it.

- Blindly follow rules and do everything by the book, even if the rules are not working.

- Fail to communicate with employees effectively yet have no inclination to learn better communication skills.

- Cultivate and maintain a network of relationships that support their co-dependent behaviors.

- Avoid, rather than resolve conflict.

- Don't develop themselves (leadership skills for example).

- Can seem very supportive, but don't teach, train or develop others through effective feedback or guidance.

- Expect others to figure out how to do the job on their own.

- Intimidated by change.

- Fail to solve problems.

- See most unforeseen events as negative and approach them with skepticism and trepidation.

- Lack perseverance in the face of challenges, but insist that others persevere.

- Lack curiosity and creativity.

Scarecrow leaders are not using their brains wisely. They are relying instead on their own emotional feedback, and because they are often emotionally immature, the feedback is erratic and unpredictable. They not only lack emotional intelligence (EQ), they also lack effective leadership skills which any thinking person can see is a formula for failure.

We Don't Think... So Neither Should You

An example of the Scarecrow's ineffective interpersonal skills is an event that occurred to an employee that tried to make a suggestion in a meeting. He prefaced the suggestion with "I think...," to which the manager quickly and curtly replied, "You're not paid to think." Immediately, the employee shut down and never again offered suggestions. He essentially disengaged his brain to survive in that organization.

This is the legacy of Scarecrow leaders. They are often the victims of other leaders with ineffective interpersonal and communicational skills and they learn early on that it isn't safe to engage their brain in the land of OZ.

Once they learn to be obedient and compliant enough, the Wizard moves them into management roles where they reproduce their own fear-based behaviors, thereby engendering entire departments where people are functioning as if they had no brains.

People who are afraid to think do very little to improve the health of an organization. What they do is allow the Wizard to continue to appear important and necessary to the organization's survival, and that's all that matters in OZ.

As long as the Wizard can maintain the illusion that employees could not function without his wisdom and power, the Board of Directors will keep praising his heroic efforts and paying him obscene amounts of money—and he can keep buying new mirrors and adding new smoke machines. The Scarecrow is just a weak pawn, but having a pawn to help pull off the ruse is always a plus to the Wizard.

CHAPTER FIVE
The Heartless Tin Man

> When a man's an empty kettle
> He should be on his mettle,
> And yet I'm torn apart.
> Just because I'm presumin'
> That I could be kind-of-human,
> If I only had a heart.
>
> The Tin Man From *The Wizard of Oz*

Like the Scarecrow, the Tin Man isn't too hard to recognize. This type of leader acts cold and hard as nails and has a stiff, unyielding demeanor. Like the Tin Man in the story of Oz, he has a heart in there somewhere, but many don't seem to know it and those who do know try very hard not to let it show. Often the heartless leader has kept his caring side hidden away for so long that he has forgotten it is even there.

In the land of OZ showing heart is greatly discouraged. Heart, the Wizard asserts, gets in the way of getting things done and of making sure they are done exactly right. According to the Wizard, the things of heart are completely unnecessary "soft skills" which the organization is better off without. Heart, OZ leaders insist, does not drive performance or add to the bottom line.

The Wizard could not be more wrong. Heart is the only thing that *does* drive performance and sustain a healthy bottom line. The fear and coercion that are part and parcel of the old school command and control style of management can keep the ball rolling for awhile, but not for long. Heartless tactics cause employees to disengage and to spend a great deal of energy protecting their territory which greatly impacts productivity. This is especially true now as the newly enlightened generations continue to refuse to take an inferior role.

The truly heartless managers have no consideration for the needs of the people in their organization. They regularly discount or altogether fail to recognize or acknowledge employee contributions. They believe that the only way to motivate people to work effectively is through fear, intimidation or shame, and they wield these like an ax ready to chop people down to size and keep them in line.

Managers of this type are certain that fear is what drives performance so they keep dishing it out. As a result, employees become unwilling to innovate, offer solutions or risk making a mistake. Trust, enthusiasm and motivation are destroyed and along with these, performance.

Tin Man leaders with hearts on ice rarely stop to consider that they may be the source of employee ineffectiveness. It is always employee "ineptness" in their opinion. If the thought of trying a new tactic like camaraderie or kindness ever crosses his mind, he doesn't let it stay there for long. He can't afford to.

The Wizard expects leaders to be tough as nails and, to meet expectations, the Tin Man keeps his heart well hidden. There's a huge cost, not just to the employees, but to the Tin Man and the organization. The Tin Man ends up with heart problems, ulcers, broken relationships and all kinds of unfortunate things and the organization ends up losing productivity and profits.

According to a study done by Sirota Survey Intelligence in June 2006, employees are as much as fifteen times more enthusiastic about their work and the organization they work for when equity, achievement and camaraderie are present in the workplace. The same study suggests that where heart is absent in the workplace, the morale of 85% of employees will decline sharply after the first 6 months on the job (Entrepreneur.com 2006).

Cold-hearted leaders, upon seeing such statistics, may give lip service to people-centric practices purely for the profit potential, but people soon see right through lip service so it never works for long. Caring and camaraderie cannot be faked. They actually *require* heart, which is a problem for the Tin Man since he has locked his away.

Silos of Protection

Where morale and trust are low, silos of protection form around individuals or small groups, and communication suffers greatly. Where communication is lacking between departments and between key people, employees become unwilling to innovate, offer solutions or risk making a mistake so huge amounts of time, money and human resources are wasted.

In our studies, employees in siloed companies estimate that they waste *three to five hours a day* trying to get information or waiting for someone else to get some essential part of the project to them. They report, typically with great frustration, that they rarely know where projects actually stand at any given time because no one is communicating.

In OZ organizations, copious e-mails copied to dozens of people, and mostly meaningless voice mails and memos pass for communication. This is *not* communication. It is generally just a collection of data that strengthens the silos of perceived safety.

The Tin Man manager can see that problems exist, but he thinks the problems can only be resolved if the employees change, and the Wizard has convinced him that they will not change without continual coercion. So the Tin Man dutifully follows the rules, never daring to consider how coercion further limits communication, strengthens silos, and destroys incentive and the productivity he pushes so hard to generate.

As productivity decreases, the Tin Man manager pushes people harder, but the focus is on compliance, systems improvement and time management, which he imagines will improve performance, but they don't really. This becomes a catch 22 for everyone. The Tin Man is attending to the wrong things and employees are mired in details, collecting data, and creating reports to pass back and forth.

All the while the Tin Man is feeling self-satisfied believing he is driving performance since the employees seem to be working very hard. In spite of all the activity, the bottom line generally doesn't improve, so the Tin Man keeps hacking away at things, and the employees keep scrambling in an effort to dodge the ax.

Bill, the CIO of an energy company, described his Tin Man boss to Julie during a coaching session. Bill has an MBA and with 23 years in management positions, has a lot of management experience under his belt, but that doesn't count for much in the OZ organization where he works.

"Every Monday morning," Bill explained, "our CFO comes to work in a bad mood. It's as though he believes a bad mood is a necessary component to being a good manager. He starts by complaining about the 'idiot' that runs marketing and demanding to know who gave so-and-so the authority to make that decision. He demands to know the intricate details and nuances of every decision anyone in the organization has dared to make. He is a master of finger pointing, yelling and constant grilling, which keeps everyone in the whole company scurrying around checking and rechecking details."

When asked how that impacted productivity, Bill replied, "It's a wonder that we make any progress at all on our larger initiatives. Yet the CFO believes any progress we do make comes about as a result of his constant driving, demanding and heartless tactics. Every Friday afternoon he pats himself on the back and, in one way or another, declares that whatever success the organization has had that week is mostly due to his 'all business' approach to getting things done.

The rest of us have found that protesting or trying to give anyone else credit is a waste of time so we just tune out and wait for him to finish. Needless to say the frustration of the entire organization continues to mount because everyone knows that, no matter what they do, it won't be good enough and it won't change the fact that every Monday morning, the madness will start all over again and that's how the week will go. The CFO thinks our turnover is high because our employees are 'idiots who don't know a good thing when they see it.' The rest of us know differently."

The "Solution" is Often the Problem

It is not uncommon for Tin Man leaders to perceive their heartless approach as the solution when in fact it is quite often the source of the problem. Heartless tactics may have worked to some degree when people didn't know that they had options, but as many organizations are discovering to their dismay, the younger generations *do* know and they are not willing to work in a heartless, soulless or mindless environment.

There are actually two types of Tin Man leaders; those who really don't like people and shouldn't be managing them at all, and those who actually have very big hearts which they have learned to shut down for protection. Those who fit the latter category are generally men who lead with feeling, but who have bought into the stereotypical idea that showing heart is a sign of weakness, and women who believe they must be tougher than nails in order to be taken seriously.

We frequently find that organizations themselves produce the Tin Man phenomenon by pushing their kinder, gentler managers (male and female) to be tougher. Typically this type of Tin Man leader wants very much to please people. They want to support and protect their team members and they want to please their superiors, which often puts them in a very difficult position when upper management insists they be tough. People with big hearts don't do "tough" very well so, to comply with the demands of their leaders, they find it necessary to shut down their feelings and the "heartless" Tin Man is born.

Just as the Tin Man in *The Wizard of Oz* was kind, but misguided and unaware, so too are many Tin Man leaders. When they have become fearful of showing their feelings in the workplace, the result is great amounts of stress which they try very hard to manage. But the stress combined with fear of getting fired if they don't comply, frequently results in the behaviors seen by others as heartless. Heartlessness is never the intent of leaders in this group, but it is often the result.

Gina recently worked with two such individuals. The first was a middle manager who reported that he was operating under a great deal of stress because upper management was "pounding" him about being too soft on his his staff. His superiors insisted that he get tough and he was trying, but his team was not responding well to the change. He was frustrated because the push back from his team had convinced him that they had "taken advantage of his soft side" and that now he had no choice but to be tougher in order to earn their respect and keep his job.

In interviewing the team, Gina discovered quite the opposite was true. The team reported that they had a great deal of respect for their leader before he suddenly changed into "Mr. Hyde." In fact, they reported that they would have followed him to the ends of the earth had he asked. They admitted that they were a bit lax at times because he had allowed it, but all agreed that had he approached them with the dilemma of upper management wanting tighter controls, they would have gladly made adjustments in support of their boss. Instead, he had become cold, distant, detached, and overly demanding, which was not providing any incentive at all and had just made bad matters worse.

Once the manager learned this, he quickly let go of the tough, cold style, which was as stressful to him as to his people, and went to work to reengage his team. With some coaching around personal boundaries, he was able to enlist his people's help in tightening some of the standards as requested by upper management without alienating his team. The team's consistently excellent performance validated the effectiveness of his gentle management style and superiors had to acknowledge that his style did work. With his team's renewed commitment to performance, and with the healthy boundaries Gina helped the leader develop, he was able to communicate with his superiors with more confidence and support his team the way he wanted to. As a result his department's productivity skyrocketed.

The second example was a female executive in a male dominated industry. She lived under constant fear that her authority would be undermined if she did not maintain a position of power at all times. She believed she had to keep anything that resembled "heart" tightly guarded or she would lose the respect of the men who worked for her. In interviewing her team,

Gina discovered that they viewed her as the typical Tin Man leader—cold, heartless, critical, and unreasonably demanding. This was not her intention at all. She was experiencing a huge amount of stress because she was not living and working true to her nature and values, and the stress was driving a lot of her behaviors. She reported that she felt like a fraud and her fear of being "discovered" was causing her to put on a false front that was not serving her, or her team, well.

With coaching she was able to let go of the judgments and expectations that she had lived by and embrace her nature. She started managing her team from a place of heart. She began allowing her team to see her true strengths and encouraged them to discover their own. Her personal transformation became the catalyst for a highly positive and productive shift that took place throughout her team and resulted in greater team cohesion and effectiveness.

As with the Tin Man in the movie, these managers had a heart all along. But, without understanding how to properly engage it, they felt cold and empty inside and that is what they projected to others. Tin Man leaders often report feeling stuck in a way that is reminiscent of the rusted position in which the Tin Man found himself in the story of Oz—completely frozen and unable to move. And, like the Tin Man in the story, these leaders often become exemplary with just a little "oiling."

Today's workforce insists on leaders with heart, so "oiling" is critically important right now. They want to work for an organization that has a grand and heartfelt vision and guiding principles that the organization clearly conveys and consistently follows. They want their work to be filled with meaning and purpose. They want to be passionate about it and, if they aren't, they have no qualms about leaving to continue their search for a place about which that they can be genuinely passionate.

The Tin Man style appeared to work during the industrial revolution, but it was only the mechanistic production model and the values of the era that allowed that model of leadership to continue. Command and control is not working today and until Tin Man leaders figure this out and adopt the authentically warm, people-centric style of which most are not only capable, but actually naturally inclined, the workforce will continue to exit OZ.

Recognizing the Tin Man Leader

- Disconnected from employees, subordinates and many of their peers to focus on appeasing superiors and shareholders.

- Disconnected from their own feelings to adhere to the corporate focus on "get it done" and "get it right."

- Use rules and requirements to justify their behaviors and ensure compliance. Don't necessarily follow the rules themselves, but insist that others do.

- Do not attempt to communicate on any meaningful level. Prefer to hide behind superiors and simply pass on orders.

- Can be intimidating and infuriating though they often fail to see this in themselves.

- Those who dislike people, tend to seek out other heartless Tin Men to validate the rightness of their lack of empathy.

- When it comes to conflict, the non-people types seek it out, glory in it, gain energy from it and use to sustain their sense of power. Their approach to conflict is "bring it on!" The people-oriented types try to avoid conflict to the point of creating it.

- Employee development focuses on job-specific technical skills that ensure the job gets done right.

- Expect others to perform their job exactly as told. Any other way is wrong. Don't motivate and inspire others. Prefer to coerce, intimidate or manipulate.

- Only embrace changes they or the company initiate. Dictate solutions rather than problem solve.

- See unforeseen situations as negative, but attack them when they occur in an attempt to control the outcome.

- Feel they need to always be calling the shots.

- Some of this type lack empathy—cannot see other people's point of view and don't really care about their employees' personal needs. Some have too much empathy and have shut it down to prevent looking "weak."

Put 'em up, Put 'em up! Which one of you first? I can fight you both together if you want. I can fight you with one paw tied behind my back. I can fight you standing on one foot. I can fight you with my eyes closed.

The Lion From *The Wizard of Oz*

CHAPTER SIX
The Cowardly Lion

In the story of Oz the Cowardly Lion put up a good front as long as there were no real challengers. When there were, he made a hasty retreat. His bravado was not meanness though; it was a façade to hide his insecurities. In reality the Cowardly Lion is a gentle, caring and even humble creature. He hides out when he can and, when he can't, he pretends to be tough to keep others from seeing his vulnerabilities.

The same is true of the Cowardly Lions in OZ organizations. Their biggest problem is that they don't have the courage to make the hard decisions and follow through on them, but they don't want anyone to know this. They reason that if they look tough enough and mean enough, no one will ever get close enough to realize they are really softies who often feel uncertain and insecure.

For the Cowardly Lion, the bravado is not about feeding a big ego as many assume. It's about hiding their frailties. They usually work very hard at maintaining the tough, intimidating image because it is actually quite foreign to their true nature. Most Cowardly Lions would really prefer to follow someone else's lead and maintain a more laid-back, easy-going pace.

They don't like conflict so try to keep a low profile and side-step sticky issues rather than face them. They avoid tough issues they really should be addressing and defer decisions to others whenever possible.

As with the heartless types, the Cowardly Lion concedes to the Wizard, but for very different reasons. Cowardly Lions tend to be tender-hearted and really do care about their people. They want to stand up for them, but lack the courage. In their case, the Wizard is frightening and they comply out of fear more than out of agreement with the Wizard's style.

Employees tend to find their Cowardly Lion managers likable when they can connect with them, but they don't respect them and don't trust them to step up to the plate when things get tough. As a result, their employees are often cautious about following their lead.

The Unofficial Leader to the Rescue—Sometimes

It is not uncommon for a bolder member of the Cowardly Lion's team to take over in a behind the scenes way and assume an unofficial leadership role, making the decisions on the manager's behalf. This unofficial leader acts as an advisor upon whom the Cowardly Lion comes to depend quite heavily.

Sometimes, the unofficial leader gets his or her needs met in that they get to be the boss without being responsible to upper management, and they hold a key role in their team. For them the psychological "paycheck" is enough. This type of employee will actually request and take on additional responsibilities to help their boss succeed. All this employee needs to keep performing well is plenty of gratitude and acknowledgement, and a few extra perks, which the Cowardly Lion is usually good about giving.

Sometimes, though, the unofficial leader comes to resent the fact that he or she has the responsibility, but not the title or the paycheck. For this individual, the financial rewards and/or positional power are important. They may request a raise and/or an official title and, if they don't get it, may actually do things to sabotage their manager.

Usually when a raise is denied it is because it is not in the budget and the manager does not have the skills or courage to negotiate a budget increase, but the aspiring leader is on a mission and doesn't care why the results don't come.

Once this type of unofficial leader decides they deserve more than they are receiving, they begin maneuvering in hopes of getting the attention of upper managers and claiming the official title and position for themselves, or they seek to leave the Cowardly Lion's team and move into a management position elsewhere.

With the help of an unofficial leader that is happy with the psychological payoffs, the Cowardly Lion can function fairly well because they have a willing and cooperative advisor to make decisions for them.

With the resentful type, the unofficial leader becomes a real problem and can wreak all sorts of havoc. Once disengaged, the unofficial leader becomes a trouble maker and goes from being the manager's confidant, advisor and cheerleader to being a sarcastic critic, resistant to any ideas that are not their own. They cajole and manipulate the Cowardly Lion manager with the intent of making him look bad so they have a better shot at the official title and position. This unofficial leader, when given the chance, often becomes a heartless Tin Man leader.

The Cowardly Lion, being a coward, tends to side-step, rather than confront the saboteur, and as the dynamics shift, any team spirit that might have existed begins to deteriorate and is soon dead.

Cowards are Easily Swayed

Cowardly Lions are easily swayed by their employees but not nearly so much as they are swayed by the more powerful and decisive leaders in the organization. All it usually takes to completely change the direction in which the Cowardly Lion's team is headed is a manager's meeting where peers or superiors suggest some alternative.

One strongly stated suggestion is often all it takes to alter the entire direction of the Cowardly Lion's thinking. Then all the time, energy and resources their team members have committed to the former directives are suddenly off the table and no longer important. Untold time and money is lost to the tidal shifts created by indecisive Cowardly Lions.

When the Cowardly Lion changes direction due to his inability to stand up to other people's opinions, and fails to defend a viable path which the team has already put blood, sweat and tears into, team members become frustrated and demoralized. They lose perspective. Their emotions are tossed around. They feel confused and once again directionless. Stress climbs and productivity drops drastically.

Stress goes up for the Cowardly Lion too, but rather than taking the courageous route and making a firm decision, he hides and the team becomes even more confused and more leaderless than ever.

When the actions of team members get the attention of upper management (and a drop in productivity and profits almost always has that effect), the result is often that the Wizard comes down on Cowardly Lion managers telling them that they have to get tougher. It is at this point that the Cowardly Lion, in trying to comply, puts on the tough act and comes out snarling—for awhile.

The tendency to bounce back and forth between being indecisive and easy-going, and acting tough and ferocious further adds to the confusion and lack of trust in employees and to the stress of the Cowardly Lion manager. Thus the vicious cycle continues to escalate—and the tornado rages on.

In our experience, Cowardly Lions are typically found in mid-management positions. They are occasionally found at the top in small companies, but usually by default. They may inherit their role from a family member or gain their position in the company as a result of being the largest stake-holder. As with all ineffective leadership styles, the higher up the organizational ladder the Cowardly Lion manages to climb, the greater the negative effect.

In *Good to Great*, the landmark book on the factors for organizational greatness, author Jim Collins points out the fact that great leaders, those Collins calls "Level 5 leaders", are humble and genuinely caring on the one hand and courageous enough to make the hard decisions on the other.

Cowardly Lions are often caring and humble. It's the courage part that trips them up. The cowardly manager may talk the talk, but because they infrequently walk the walk, trust is low and confusion high in their team.

Caring Without Courage

Like the lion in the Land of Oz, the corporate coward challenges others with clichés until confronted. Then, in the face of confrontation backs down and becomes a coward.

Here is an example: a valuable and conscientious employee is being directly impacted by a difficult employee that is regularly disrupting the entire team. The conscientious employee brings this to the attention of the manager and requests intervention. The disruptive employee clearly needs to be managed, but the Cowardly Lion hands the responsibility off to the complaining employee with, "You guys need to figure out a way to work it out."

With this kind of manager, employees are at a loss as to how to circumvent problems. Their only recourse is to complain to a superior, which generally just makes the employee look petty. Most employees realize this and most organizations have policies in place that prevent it. Going over a manager's head is a difficult and risky thing in OZ organizations so the Cowardly Lion can fly under the radar for a very long time. Problems generally emerge only when employee turnover becomes unusually high and that can take a long time because the Cowardly Lion's humble, caring demeanor makes employees feel guilty for being frustrated with his or her short-comings.

Employees doubt that this manager will ever have their back should something go wrong and, with projects constantly shifting at the whim of every superior, they eventually come to doubt that their hard work will ever result in anything worthwhile either. Under the management of a

Cowardly Lion it doesn't take long for an entire team to lose all interest in performing.

On the other hand employees don't know what to do with the fact that this is a basically nice, though effete manager. Unless one of the employees decides to step up to the plate, start making decisions and guide the manager toward team goals, the team remains directionless and frustrated. Typically, the employees of Cowardly Lions only report their frustrations during exit interviews.

Recognizing Cowardly Lions

- Appear to be in agreement with superiors and will easily acquiesce to their suggestions and demands, but don't often follow through. Like a weather vain in the wind, their focus points in whatever direction the leader of the moment suggests.

- May privately disagree with the position of their superior, yet will publicly agree and even seem enthusiastic about the initiative, but will rarely actually carry the enthusiasm forward.

- When it comes to rules, does not want to look like the bad guy, but will play the game when superiors are watching. When superiors are not watching will defer compliance of rules to team members or an unofficial leader on their team.

- Empathetic listeners who really would like to help their team succeed, but are afraid of their superiors, so often come across as tough at times and easy-going at times leaving employees confused.

- Tend to have a few close friends and confidants, but do not have a strong network of people. Tend to protect their position by maintaining distance.

- Avoid conflict and will hand it off to any willing volunteer.

- Open to learning and developing themselves as leaders, but in OZ organizations, the assertiveness training they need to be more effective is often not made available.

- Very open to employee development. Understand that effective employees make them look better.

- Open to allowing their employees to perform their work in their own way. Tends to encourage rather than coerce.

- Try to motivate employees by encouraging them and allowing them to decide for themselves. This typically backfires and leads to frustration rather than motivation.

- Greatly dislike change, which is anxiety producing for them. Intimidated by the new and different.

- Defer problem-solving to others. This is not delegation, but deference. Others are allowed to decide how the problem should be solved.

- When it comes to meeting challenges, theirs is leadership by abdication. They find meeting challenges draining and avoid it.

- Lack assertiveness skills, which is an essential and always learned skill. They are not naturally bold and need training to help them manage the fear that conflict brings up.

The big impact of Cowardly Lions and all other ineffective managers will hit harder and harder as Generation X and Millennials become the primary workforce because they are quick to change situations they are unhappy with. These generations won't put up with something they see is not working for very long. They will simply walk out and start looking for other options; other departments to which they can move or for another company altogether.

The Cowardly Lion is one of the most easily redirected of all ineffective management types because they really do care about how they impact people. With the right training, they can be excellent managers and just the kind of leader the new workforce is looking for.

CHAPTER SEVEN
Lions and Tigers and Bears, Oh My!

Too often, when OZ organizations are going through change (and they almost always are), the process is quite scary and unpredictable. Because communication is frequently lacking in OZ organizations, employees are left in the dark through much of the change process. They have no idea what to expect so they become very cautious and vigilant about moving forward.

Managers who would love to do a good job and help their people move through the change process effectively are generally as frustrated as their employees, and usually just as fearful because they can't get any answers either.

Because the Wizard likes to keep things hidden, there are times when even the company's senior level executives have no clear idea as to where the organization is headed, exactly why it is going there, or what to expect. So when employees go to their managers seeking solace, they have none to give and both the executive and the employees are left feeling less secure.

For employees and managers alike, moving through an uncertain and constantly changing environment where nothing is clear feels like a long trek through a deep, dark forest without the aid of a compass or guide.

In OZ organizations everyone is expected to follow the rules and directives (the Wizard's version of the Yellow Brick Road) without question. But, in the middle of a dark, scary forest, when unforeseen things keep jumping out at you and your teammates are falling by the wayside, it's hard to trust those who keep urging you on, telling you things will turn out fine if you just stay on the path they have prescribed. It's much easier, and seemingly wiser, to expect the worst and proceed very cautiously—or not at all.

Failure to provide a clear vision and a trustworthy environment to help employees move through change successfully costs employers billions of dollars each year. In fear laden environments, vigilant employees are far too busy watching their backs to engage fully in anything the organization considers important.

The Engagement Challenge

Gallup studies done in 2000, 2004 and 2008 estimate that disengaged employees are costing employers more than 300 billion dollars annually on average, and the cost increases year after year. Polls taken every few years show that, without exception, engaged employees make up less than a third of the workforce.

The Gallup organization defines "engaged" employees (27%) as those who work with passion and feel a profound connection to their organization and its goals. They are the ones who drive innovation and move the organization forward.

"Not-engaged" employees (56%) are defined as those who show up and participate to whatever extent is essential, but who are primarily just serving their time and doing only what is necessary to keep their job and collect their paycheck. They bring no passion or energy to their work and work at a greatly diminished capacity.

"Actively disengaged" employees (17%) are unhappy with the work they do, with the organization and/or with its leadership. Both satisfaction and trust levels are very low. Not only does this group do as little as possible on the job, they actively sabotage the efforts of other employees and the goals of the organization. They regularly express and act out their unhappiness at work, visiting their misery and negative attitude on everyone around them and undermining the efforts of their more engaged colleagues.

The Gallup poll numbers in 2000 showed that engaged employees made up 29% of the workforce, 55% were not engaged and 16% were actively disengaged. In 2004 the numbers were: engaged 26%, not engaged 55%, actively disengaged 19%. In 2008 the numbers were engaged employees 27%, not engaged 56%, and actively disengaged 17% (Gallup 2008). Clearly things are not getting any better and it is costing organizations plenty.

James K. Clifton, Chairman and CEO of the Gallup Organization, in an article entitled *Employee Engagement: A Leading Indicator of Financial Performance* says, "Actively disengaged employees erode an organization's bottom line while breaking the spirits of colleagues in the process. Within the U.S. workforce, Gallup estimates this cost to be more than $300 billion in lost productivity alone."

Mike Johnson, author of *The New Rules of Engagement*, pretty much sums up why the disengaged employee numbers have remained relatively steady and are on the rise in OZ organizations. Johnson wrote, "Of course we've been really good at disengaging our employees these last years. We've spent millions in consulting fees to find ways to cut our employees' pensions and health benefits (now there's disengagement for you) and then we say we want you to be part of our brand. We've fired thousands of people after mergers and sell-offs and our websites proclaim that one of our goals is to be an employer of choice. We've cut personal and professional development programs to the bone and then we expect our employees to be up-to-speed and enthusiastic."

Employees who lack trust in the organization they work for, or in their leaders, will continue to be vigilant, and vigilant employees cannot get past their fears and concerns even if they want to. And most *do* want to.

Lost Hours

Based on our employee interviews, ineffective leadership is probably costing organizations far more than what the Gallop polls indicate. Confidential interviews of thousands of employees over the past twelve years revealed that the average amount of time lost every single day to confusion and lack of communication averages 2.5 hours per employee.

The estimates of lost time and productivity cited here are *employee-based estimates*, not management estimates, and they come from in-person interviews with employees whose estimates might actually be less than the reality. Some have given estimates as high as four hours, half of their day, and almost all of them are frustrated because of it. With this happening on a regular basis in organizations all across the country, the real cost is probably in the trillions.

Management is typically shocked and appalled when they hear the hours wasted figures. Many deny that this is the case in their organization, and not surprisingly. In OZ organizations, the reasons are discounted or completely ignored and generally remain unaddressed. Why? Because the reasons given typically point to poor leadership.

They Include:

- Bottlenecks created by inadequate information or resources
- Lack of direction
- Lack of concern for employee's needs
- Inane requests
- Organizational blunders
- Poor communication
- Secrecy or lack of transparency
- Lack of cooperation between departments

Employees typically boil the reasons down to three things:

1. Leaders don't care (lack heart)

2. Leaders are incompetent (have disengaged brains)

3. Leaders refuse to admit that they don't know everything and ask for help when they clearly need it (lack the courage to be vulnerable and authentic)

The third item (lack of courage) covers a broad spectrum. Besides the courage to admit that they don't know everything, this category includes the courage to open themselves to opportunities to learn, grow and improve their skills rather than thinking they have arrived and already know everything. It includes the courage to make hard decisions when they are the right decisions, the courage to ask the people in the trenches for information and feedback, and the courage to show up authentically rather than hiding behind a façade of bravado.

Keeping Up Appearances

Frank Baum, the author of *The Wizard of Oz*, had a talent for seeing beyond the façades and putting a face and character to human frailties. And producer, Victor Fleming, brought them to brilliant life in the film.

The Scarecrow, Tin Man and Cowardly Lion characters fit the characters of the three most frequently named ineffective managers in uncanny ways. And the Wizard effectively describes top executives that prefer to keep the smoke and mirrors in place to avoid admitting that they are fallible human beings and need help just like the rest of us.

As was so appropriately portrayed in the book and film, none of these characters were really bad underneath their disguises. The only truly bad character was the Wicked Witch of the West whom we will examine in the next chapter. All the others only had to discover their truth to claim the attributes they sought; attributes they had all along, but of which they were unaware. We frequently find that to be the case in OZ organizations too. It's why we hold the belief that the problems so many organizations face today can be resolved through three simple things: willingness to learn and grow, deeper awareness and understanding, and commitment to cooperative solutions.

The only place we run into seemingly unsolvable problems in OZ organizations is where the Wizard and the Witch have formed an alliance and created a fortress around it.

Though the Wizard and the Witch were not associated in the book or film, in OZ organizations they frequently feed off one another in their quest for power.

As you will discover in the next chapter, Witches are masters at starting fires and fanning flames and Wizards are masters at using those flames to generate lots of smoke.

The two together are more than just scary, they can be downright dangerous, wreaking havoc across entire organizations. These two in concert are generally the source of the mounting tension and stress that employees report and of the consistently high levels of disengagement. They drive the secrecy that keeps employees in the dark and fearful of change initiatives.

As long as secrecy and fear are the tactics leaders use to drive performance, employees will cautiously inch forward at best. This has always been true. It is the nature of fear. But the consequences of such an approach are far greater today than they used to be. More than ever before employees forced to move into a place of uncertainty and fear are choosing to leave the organization and go in search of a brighter future, and the cost to organizations is astronomical.

In today's fast paced world, organizations cannot afford to move forward by mere inches and they certainly cannot afford to lose their best and brightest employees.

Change is rarely easy, but it can be much easier than most organizations make it. The way to make it easier is to address the real issues. Employees need to know why change is occurring and they need to believe that it will in some way improve current conditions. If leaders cannot convey that to everybody in the organization—*everybody*—and back it up with action, they will continue to lose their best and brightest employees.

Staying transparent and keeping employees fully informed may not make all of them enjoy the change process more, but it will certainly help them navigate it better and with far greater effectiveness.

CHAPTER EIGHT
Beware the Wicked Witch and Flying Monkeys

> Just try and stay out of my way.
> Just try! I'll get you, my pretty
> and your little dog too!
>
> The Wicked Witch
> From *The Wizard of Oz*

In OZ organizations zeal can adversely affect entire groups of people and when it does, these people become like the flying monkeys in *The Wizard of Oz*. They blindly follow orders and adapt to the dysfunctions of the environment.

If the environment is hostile, they become hostile. If the boss is unreasonable, they become unreasonable too. If the prescribed code of conduct is mindless, heartless or lacking in courage, they follow suit and behave in kind. If the organization is too lax or too strict, so are the Monkeys. If those in leadership positions are so frustrated, overworked, fearful, bitter or angry much of the time that they become negative and, like the Wicked Witch, seek to visit their negativity on others, the Flying Monkeys follow the Witch's lead and treat people equally poorly.

With an army of Flying Monkeys to do their bidding, the few who are brave enough to stand up to the hostility of Witch-like leaders are quickly brought down. Hostile work environments affect an organization's effectiveness far more than is generally openly acknowledged. Low employee morale, absenteeism, high turnover and low productivity can be the outward signs of an organization that is not paying attention to negative leadership styles. But where there is a leader bent on terrorizing employees into submission, few employees will dare to act out openly or express their views.

In organizations or departments run by tyrants who surround themselves with informants, employees quickly discover that everything eventually finds its way back to the tyrant and that there are always consequences.

Even employee surveys and 360 feedback reports will usually not reflect the problems unless the employees are completely convinced that the candid reports can never be traced back to them. That is rarely the case though, because 360 assessments are typically administered by department, and managers don't generally have so many employees that they can't figure out who reported what.

Sometimes employees won't report the truth because they fear for themselves and sometimes it is because they fear retribution against the entire team should one member be so bold as to express concern or give the Witch manager a bad review.

The Performance Barometer

Employee morale is always the barometer for how well leadership is performing. Unhealthy environments always result in low morale and, where a tyrant is running the show, morale is often so low and the atmosphere so negative as to be palpable.

As organizational consultants, trainers and coaches, each of the authors has had occasion to visit organizations, or units within organizations, where low morale and fear are immediately evident. In some instances, the workplace atmosphere is so heavy as to be oppressive. Where we have had the opportunity to conduct confidential interviews with employees in such environments, they always validate the low morale we have readily observed.

The big questions is, if an outsider can detect low morale in one visit, how is it that leaders who are there day in and day out miss it? The answer, of course, is that the leaders of OZ organizations are not looking at their employees. They are focused on the bottom line and on pleasing the Great Wizard.

The Three Toxic Cultures

No-Mistakes - There are three cultures that commonly occur in OZ organizations and none of them are healthy. One is a "no mistakes" culture where everyone is expected to follow every rule perfectly and precisely. There is no flexibility in this culture. Employees must get to work at the precise time the organization requires, take breaks only when scheduled and follow the procedures manual to the letter. To come in late or make any kind of mistake is to be called out and humiliated in front of peers. The result of this rigid approach is a fear paralyzed workforce that doesn't dare do anything new or innovative.

By its very nature, innovation is a process of trial and error which means mistakes will occur. They are to be expected. But in a no-mistakes culture, mistakes are unacceptable and are not tolerated, so employees soon learn not to try new things. They cling fearfully to the tried and true, even if it isn't working.

This culture is very common in organizations where Witches are in positions of power. The other two cultures, while not generally a direct result of the Witch's style, are often spawned in departments or divisions as a backlash or in response to the Witch's frightening style, especially when the Witch has the blessings of the Wizard.

No-Consequence - The second toxic culture is a "no-consequence" culture. On the surface, this culture doesn't appear toxic. It appears to be a rather laid-back, easy-going environment. What it really is though, is an environment where everyone, including managers, has become too disengaged to care.

We will cover the no-consequence culture in the next chapter because that is not the type of culture we find in tyrannical environments where the Witch rules. What we typically find here is a no-mistakes culture, or a fire-fighter culture—the third toxic culture.

Fire-fighter - In a no-mistakes culture, employees are damned if they do and damned if they don't. There is no way to win. In a fire-fighter culture, employees feel lost and directionless, yet harried and overworked. There is always more work than there are hands to perform it or time to fit it all into.

Department heads in a fire-fighter culture are so covered up with busy work and trying to keep the department profitable so the Witch isn't screaming or the Wizard doesn't eliminate them, that they have little time to actually manage their people. Fire-fighter managers tend to take on too many tasks that really should be delegated, so they are as overworked and frazzled as their employees. And they often take their frustrations out on the employees even when they don't really mean to.

Managers forced into a fire-fighter culture often report that they do so much of the work themselves because they recognize that their employees are already overworked and largely disengaged. They are either trying to take some of the burden off their employees' shoulders or they do not think the employees can be trusted to follow through on projects without direct supervision. And, of course, they are too busy to take the time to communicate fully or to supervise other people's projects so projects frequently don't get done correctly or on time. This adds to the conviction that fire-fighting is the only option and it continues.

When it is suggested that a different leadership style would get them far better results in less time and with less effort, few fire-fighters are willing to believe that. They can't imagine that the employees they have could be engaged and effective without their direct supervision. They don't believe that the employees whose slack they are regularly taking up could possibly complete a project from beginning to end on their own. And in a fire-fighter culture they can't. They don't have the means to. Yet it has been our experience that any team can become a high performance team when given the right tools and conditions.

Usually that requires some training and coaching for both the leader and their employees, and it may even require some shifting around of employees, but even the worst of teams can become excellent ones given the right tools, training and environment.

A testimonial from one of my clients, a large international corporation, points to this reality. The client wrote:

"As Director of Employee Training and Organizational Development for my company I have used Dr. Buffington's services on numerous occasions. The results have always validated why her services are so valuable to the success of our employees, executives and the company in general.

During one of our most memorable and effective engagements Sherry and her team were asked to help turn one of our most important, yet least effective and highly dysfunctional organizations around. In a relatively short period of time the assistance and guidance she provided to the organization and my department resulted in a complete and phenomenal turnaround.

Customers, who once complained, now routinely comment on the effective way employees support them. Attrition was reduced to zero, employee morale significantly improved and effectiveness went through the roof."

This was not an unusual team nor is this an unusual result. The vast majority of people really do want to do a good job—and will if given the right conditions. Unfortunately, those who lead fire-fighter cultures rarely think they can afford the time to learn how to create the right conditions.

There are just too many fires to put out. And, guess what? Until their methods change, there always will be.

The Cost of Culture Clash

The disengagement that occurs in each of these dysfunctional environments can be seen in all bureaucracies. In government run organizations and those that do contract work for the government, the no-mistakes culture clashes with the no-consequence culture on a regular basis. The result is extremely low productivity and extremely high waste.

In these organizations people move at a snail's pace because they know they won't be fired unless they do something really horrible (the no-consequence side of the equation). All they have to do is follow procedure and not vary from it one iota (the no-mistakes side). Employees in these completely dysfunctional cultures don't dare consider, much less question, whether there is a better way or suggest that there might be. They learn very quickly that independent thinking and innovation only cause problems. So they numb themselves out and simply plod through the prescribed motions.

Never mind that the procedures manuals they follow were written a hundred years ago and don't apply to today's reality. Never mind that captive customers are frustrated and angry. And never mind that it takes four people to do the job of one, or that the operation is costing tax payers ten times what it should. Plodding along slowly is the only safe way to proceed in this toxic environment, so that is exactly what happens.

In non-government organizations, where the no-mistakes culture more often rules, employees are equally disengaged and mindlessly following the rules. One would think that having employees walk the chalk line and follow the rules without question would make Witch managers happy. But, no; in organizations that need to make a profit, not getting things done effectively and efficiently, and not innovating is a mistake too. So, when the slow pace of numbed out employees and the lack of vision and innovation inflates costs and causes the organization to become obviously inefficient, as it must, the Wizard lets the Witch know that he is not happy and that something must change. The Witch then points a bony finger at the people and they get called out for their lack of innovation. A few heads roll, which temporarily frightens the remaining employees into action and they—with fear and trepidation—follow the new marching orders and try to innovate.

Then, oops! A mistake gets made and the Witch can't have mistakes! So those brave souls that stepped out there to try to meet the new directives, take the brunt of the Witch's ire and jump back in line—and the bureaucracy lumbers on.

The best employees; those who are, by nature, innovators and could actually produce the desired effect if they had any latitude, generally have a hard time staying numbed out. So they either innovate and make the mistakes—and get fired for it—or they leave in search of a better environment.

SHRM, the Society for Human Resource Management, estimates that it costs $3,500 to replace one $8 per hour employee when all costs—recruiting, interviewing, hiring, training, reduced productivity, et cetera, are considered. And SHRM's estimate is actually the *lowest* of 17 nationally respected companies who calculate this cost!

Other sources suggest that employee replacement costs 50% of the annual salary of entry-level employees, 150% of mid-level employees, and up to 400% for specialized, high level employees! And that is before factoring for job complexity.

If a job is simple, like making hamburgers, a replacement can be trained in a few days, but if the job is complex it can take several years for a new employee to reach the level of competency that a previous long time employee had reached. In this case, the cost of getting a new employee up to speed can be immense.

Bureaucracies and other OZ organizations don't consider that they are driving the high turnover rates they experience. They typically chalk it up to fickle employees, or natural attrition, or the active mining of employees by other organizations; to anything in fact, but their own poor practices. In OZ organizations employee turnover is seen as just "the cost of doing business." But oh, the cost!

Recognizing the Witch

- Their relationship with superiors tends to look more like collusion than cooperation.
- Believe all of life is a win/lose proposition and they are determined to be the winner.
- Tend to tell their superiors what they want to hear and then do whatever they please.
- When things go wrong, as they often do, they find a subordinate they can sacrifice as a scapegoat.

- Live on the negative end of the spectrum so their reactions tend to be negative – anger, frustration, blame, a false sense of injustice, etc.
- They love rules and use them as weapons, not just to control, but to inflict pain and suffering.
- Communication is non-existent except to issue orders to their minions and underlings so the underlings will do the dirty work and the Witch can stay above the fray.
- Build a pseudo-network through fear and intimidation. People comply to avoid being the target of the Witch's ire.
- Use conflict to their advantage. Set one person against another to ensure everyone is off-balance, on edge, compliant and blind to the Witch's behaviors.
- Avoid personal development and any suggestion of it. Their behaviors are based in low self-esteem and they are terrified that this fact may come out in training.
- Employee development is a process of fire and replace. They believe employees should walk in the door with every necessary capability.
- Employees cannot make mistakes and there are no second chances. Perform or get fired.
- Believe that people are naturally lazy and only perform when coerced. Any "motivation" is negative motivation, such as humiliation and threats.
- Have a long memory for mistakes and always seek pay back.
- Use change as a way to keep people unsettled and unsure so their commands are less likely to be questioned. Use change as a fear inducer and manipulation device.
- Do not handle problems themselves. They issue orders to others in a "go take care if this" manner and then punish the poor soul who gets chosen for the job if it isn't done properly.
- Meet challenges by manipulating their "monkeys". They are always willing to send the troops into battle, but never willing to go in themselves. Then if failure occurs, the troops can be blamed.
- Don't see personal development as at all necessary. They think they already know all they need to know. Their position is that if they don't already know it, it has no value. They see "soft skills" (how to work effectively with people) as valueless and will rarely invest in the development of them.

Witches are so nasty because they lack what all the other ineffective leaders lack combined. They lack heart, they lack the intellectual brain power to examine alternatives and make better decisions, and they lack the courage to do the right thing. With Witch-like bureaucrats at the helm in many governmentally run organizations, it is no wonder that government spending is out of control and the entire nation is at risk.

We can all see it, but not many people are willing to risk pushing change through. They see the outcomes of those who have tried. The Monkeys (often called boards of directors or legislators) swarm in, overwhelm the pioneers and either capture and subdue them, or push them out the door. With a vicious army of Flying Monkeys to do the Witch's bidding, the few who are brave enough to confront the Witch are quickly brought down, and those remaining go back to business as usual. That is likely to change as the socially connected Millennials begin pushing a new, more people friendly agenda.

The suggestion made by Arianna Huffington, of *The Huffington Post* in January 2010 is a precursor to what we can expect as enlightened rebels take center stage. In response to the greed and irresponsible actions taken by the large financial institutions after the government bailed them out because they were "too large to allow to fail," Huffington went on the internet and on national television suggesting that people take their money out of these large institutions and open accounts with the small regional banks that were left to survive on their own through the economic debacle, and which were acting more responsibly. And many people did just that.

Similar advice is being circulated through other sources as well; everything from online forums, to talk show hosts, to best selling authors are advising people to refuse to do business with companies that take advantage of employees and/or customers. And it doesn't stop there. People are being advised to refuse to re-elect congressmen and senators that are interested only in keeping their jobs and to support only companies and legislators that are socially, environmentally and globally responsible. The socially responsible Gen Xers and Millennials are taking it all to heart too. Change is coming folks. Get ready!

CHAPTER NINE
The Poppy Effect

While the world of entrepreneurs and independent contractors is in full bloom and abuzz with activity, OZ corporations are having a completely different experience. High performing employees are exiting in droves. Internal tension and stress are high and turnover is even higher. Employee dissatisfaction and disengagement are as high as they have ever been and getting higher. If these organizations want to survive, the new realities need to be addressed, and *soon*. People are checking out in record numbers and they are not all leaving the organizations *physically*. Many remain in body. They just check out mentally and emotionally.

As you may recall, the poppy field in *The Wizard of Oz*, while appealing, had a negative effect on those passing through it which made them want to give up their quest, lay down and just go to sleep.

Big, high powered OZ organizations look pretty appealing too from a distance, but as with the poppy field, once inside employees often find conditions that cause them to lose interest, disengage and, in effect, sleep their way through their days on the job.

There are many things that cause potentially good employees to lose interest. One pervasive factor is the no-consequence culture where disengaged managers tolerate problem employees rather than trying to find and implement effective ways to manage and motivate them.

Problematical employees require a great deal of a manager's time and, for disengaged managers, it is just easier to ignore them than to deal with them. Unfortunately, the longer managers tolerate sub-standard work and negative behaviors, the worse they tend to become.

In time, greater and greater percentages of the organization's employees begin adjusting their productivity levels downward to the lowest level tolerated and, before long, the majority of employees are simply riding the time-clock, collecting their paychecks, and doing just enough to stay out of serious trouble. Even potentially excellent employees function at less than half of their capacity in such an environment—for awhile. When things get too intolerable, the better ones leave.

In companies where under-performing employees are tolerated, potentially good, productive employees first become aggravated and their first line of action is to report the slackers to their superiors, hoping the problem will be resolved.

When managers fail to respond in a timely and appropriate way (which disengaged managers tend to do), and the slackers continue to have no consequences for their behaviors, the once productive employees become discouraged and demotivated. It is at this point that conscientious workers disengage and start looking for another employer.

The Entitlement Mindset

In no-consequence cultures an entitlement mindset develops among the ranks and can spread throughout the organization like the plague. Once employees believe they are entitled to a paycheck simply for showing up, how much they actually produce while in the workplace becomes irrelevant. Organizations then find themselves paying for warm bodies instead of sharp minds and productivity. Once productivity drops, getting the necessary work done requires more and more people—or more and more coercion.

Managers create no-consequence cultures when they are, themselves, disengaged and continual coercion from upper management tends to have that effect. Although it can be argued that employees, and especially those in positions of management, should bear responsibility for their choices and actions, for the most part their shortcomings are not premeditated or even conscious.

Though staying engaged is often difficult for almost everyone in OZ organizations, those at management levels are generally trying very hard to stay engaged to meet the needs of their employees. But, because they don't know why the employees keep disengaging and figuratively (and sometimes literally) falling asleep on the job, they are at a loss as to how to correct the problem, so the Wizard and his entourage keep hammering.

It's easy to blame the employees or to point fingers at management, and OZ leaders are usually quick to do that, but the employees are not completely at fault, and often neither are the supervisors and middle managers. It's those darn poppies!

So, what is it about the "poppies" and how do they show up in OZ organizations? The poppies represent the endless rules, both written and unwritten that are outdated and out of touch with the needs of the people. They are the spoken and unspoken expectations that are similarly unmindful of human realities and unconcerned with human needs and desires. They are the unexamined routines, such as endless reports, frequent meetings and adherence to ancient protocol, that continue to be required even though they make no sense and actually have a negative effect.

When organizational policies, rules, routines and expectations don't make sense, managers have a very hard time buying into them and convincing employees that they should be followed.

Today's employees, including many in management positions, resist following routines, procedures, and policies that don't consider human needs. And, to cope with the frustrations, they simply disengage. It's the only way they can continue to show up and at least half-way do the job.

The unenforceable rules and outdated, out of touch policies and routines in combination with lack of personal conviction and uncooperative employees is what finally leads to disengaged management. Once management disengages and the no-consequence culture develops, the entire organization begins a slow (and sometimes not so slow) decline.

Group Dynamics

To understand how an entire organization can be impacted by a too lax environment in even a few key departments, it is useful to understand group dynamics. Studies of how people behave in groups point to several factors that can negatively impact organizations and lead to the Poppy Effect.

One factor is a common phenomenon called "group-think". Group-think is the tendency of an entire group to obligingly follow the thinking and lead of one or two people in the group without questioning the wisdom of the thinking, and without openly challenging it. The more influential the "leaders" are, the more likely it is that they will not be questioned or challenged. What's more, those who take lead positions are often *not* the official leaders, especially in no-consequence cultures. The leader is often an outraged employee that has decided the only way to get things done is to do it him or herself.

Group-think results from the human need for inclusion and acceptance. Where employees are disengaged from the company's purpose, mission and goals, they are often able to show up to work every day, not for the company, but because they identify with their team.

In OZ organizations, it is not uncommon for employees and even managers to not know the company's purpose, mission, and goals. And, when this information is lacking, no one understands how their job and daily tasks contribute to anything they consider meaningful so there is no motivation to do anything for the organization. There may be motivation to stay aligned with the immediate team however.

The Induction Principle

Team spirit can be a valuable asset or a terrible detriment depending on the direction it takes. Whether group-think leads the group in a positive direction or a negative one has a lot to do with the direction set by the leader, but it is also influenced by a second phenomenon which affects almost all people. The principles behind this phenomenon are similar to the principles of heat induction.

In heat induction, if a warm object is placed next to a cold one, the cold object will draw the heat from the warm one. After awhile, both objects will be the same temperature, but the mean temperature will be much closer to the original temperature of the cold object than to the original temperature of the warm one because energy gets lost in the transfer.

The same is true when you put positive, productive people side-by-side with negative, unproductive ones in a no-consequence culture. The negative, unproductive ones soon sap the energy and enthusiasm from the productive ones and in time the entire group is functioning at minimal levels. This is especially true when the ratio of unproductive to productive workers is close to equal or when one of the negative ones assumes a leadership role. Even when the slackers are in the minority, the positive to negative drain tends to occur where the negative ones have no consequences for their behaviors.

Blending

Another very common phenomenon, called blending, occurs among groups as a result of the same forces that drive group-think; the innate human need for inclusion and acceptance. Some people think blending is an extension of group-think, but it manifests very differently. In group-think everyone just follows along blindly. In blending, group members try to fit in by matching the general behaviors and attitudes of the majority. If they can't comfortably fit the prevailing culture, they eventually find a way to abandon the group. This phenomenon can be seen in groups of all kinds, among all social classes, in every kind of society, and in every generation.

In the workplace, it works like this: if the majority of employees in an organization are positive, productive and responsible, and if that behavior is supported and rewarded, negative, irresponsible employees eventually either shape up or leave the organization of their own accord because they don't fit into the prevailing culture. They don't feel like they belong.

Unfortunately, just the opposite is true too, and to an even greater extent because of the positive to negative induction principle mentioned earlier. Because negative people tend to drain the energies of positive ones, a group often does not need anywhere near a majority on the negative side to eventually create a negative effect.

Negative Drain

In a mostly negative environment it is the positive, productive employees, those that have pride in their work and want to do a good job, who feel out of place. The stronger their work ethic and the higher their integrity, the more likely they are to leave an organization where mediocrity is the norm in search of a more suitable environment.

In time only the employees who have learned to stay mentally and emotionally asleep on the job remain in organizations with negative environments.

I once interviewed an employee that had been working at an aircraft manufacturing company for about three months. He told me that when he first started the job he was really excited about it and jumped into his work enthusiastically. Within the first week four different employees, in observing his highly productive behaviors, had approached him and told him to slow down because he was "going to work himself out of a job". This didn't deter him from working diligently at first, but by the third week the original four and several other employees had made it clear that he either slow down or they would make his life as miserable as his diligent work was likely to make theirs. To fit in, he slowed his pace, but to do it he had to disengage and he was not a happy employee. After just three months he was looking for another place to work. Even though the job he had paid quite well, the money was not as important as his integrity and work ethic.

Where was the supervisor in all this? Disengaged and mostly absent. Where were senior leaders that should care whether employees are working at half their capacity and coercing others to do the same? In their ivory towers so completely disconnected that they didn't even know this was happening, or care. Why didn't they care? Because this was one of those government contractors that had managed to convince the government that their overblown budget was necessary so, like their employees, they had no consequence for their poor performance and lack of effectiveness. No wonder we hear stories of the government paying $500 for a $6 hammer!

This kind of waste is not confined to the U.S. government and their suppliers either. It is rampant in governmental organizations on every level, from local to national, and in many large corporations. And, whether as taxpayers or consumers, we pay for all of it.

We may not have a lot of choice when it comes to how our taxes are used other than to keep voting out the slackers and wasters, but as consumers we do have a choice not to buy the products of companies when poor leadership and ineffective practices drive prices too high. And, when consumers stop buying, organizations either have to shape up or die.

In today's fast-paced, high-stakes marketplace, no company can afford under-performing employees who feel the company owes them a paycheck no matter how poorly they perform. Certainly, no company knowingly hires poor performers, so how is it that so many organizations end up with them and how can it be changed?

Organizations end up with poor performers largely by *creating* them. We have seen more instances of star performers and high potentials being reduced to burned out and struggling employees than we can even begin to count.

Real and Lasting Change Must Start at the Top

There is an answer to the performance dilemma, but leaders need to focus on the right things to get to it. It is pretty common knowledge that any real and lasting change must begin with top management and filter down from there. What is not so commonly presented is a workable solution that concerned and caring leaders can adopt.

I suspect there are many leaders that would be delighted to affect positive change if they just knew how. More often than not, when they go seeking help, what they get is advice on implementing new systems, devising new training and developing new and improved tracking methods. None of these measures will get them the results they want if the problem is disengaged employees.

The first step must be to reengage and reenergize the workforce, which is a lot easier to do than most OZ leaders imagine. Before they can do it, however, they have to get from behind the curtain and get real.

Sleeping employees are not always recognized as being asleep by disconnected leaders because the employees are going through the motions. They show up for work most of the time and seem to keep busy. But sleeping employees are always partially or fully disengaged from their work and, though they may be completing tasks when necessary, they are exerting minimal effort in the process so task completion often takes a lot longer than it should. That is to be expected when employees lose interest in the company and cease to care about doing a better job.

The Wrong Focus

When OZ leaders finally recognize that employees are under-performing and threats don't help, usually the first thing they do is provide employees with some form of training. After all, the employees are the ones under-performing, right? It can't possibly be that the environment the OZ leader has created or the leader him or herself is the problem. No. It has to be the employees. They need stricter discipline and more training.

The problem is, the leaders are focusing on the wrong things. If the hiring process was performed anywhere near correctly, meaning the candidate turned in an application and went through an interview and background check, the problem is *not* lack of technical know-how, it is lack of interest.

A study done in 2006 and reported on by Chief Learning Officer magazine suggests that in most organizations' in-class training gets satisfactory results in only 20% of those who participate. That figure includes technical training as well as soft skills training. Because of this poor statistic, organizations keep looking for new and better training, keep forging down that same worn path, and keep getting the same poor results (Whitney 2006).

In the Croft-Baker study conducted for Motorola in 2001 the results of online, self-paced training looked even bleaker. In that study, 60% of employees who registered for e-learning never even *started* their training and fewer than 25% of those who did start finished it. That factors to a completion rate of only about 10% of online learners.

According to a study conducted by Dave Zielinski in 2000, 75-80% of employees that begin e-learning courses never finish them. The problem is not necessarily the training itself but the fact that intrinsic motivation and comprehension are lacking (Zielinski 2000).

I developed the matrix below to help explain why training will never get organizations the results they are seeking until they have created conditions that keep employees interested and engaged. The matrix was developed after years of research led me to realize why training, as organizations typically provide it, gets such poor results

The Performance Matrix

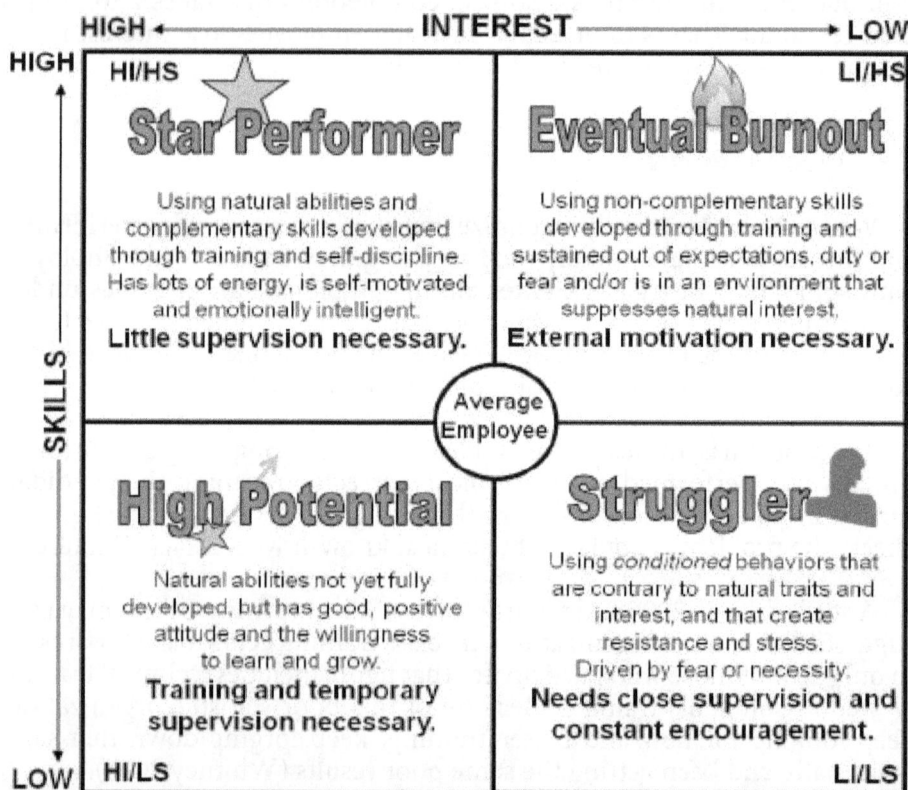

HIGH ◄─────────── INTEREST ───────────► LOW

HI/HS — ⭐ **Star Performer**
Using natural abilities and complementary skills developed through training and self-discipline. Has lots of energy, is self-motivated and emotionally intelligent. **Little supervision necessary.**

LI/HS — **Eventual Burnout**
Using non-complementary skills developed through training and sustained out of expectations, duty or fear and/or is in an environment that suppresses natural interest. **External motivation necessary.**

Average Employee

High Potential
Natural abilities not yet fully developed, but has good, positive attitude and the willingness to learn and grow. **Training and temporary supervision necessary.**
HI/LS

Struggler
Using *conditioned* behaviors that are contrary to natural traits and interest, and that create resistance and stress. Driven by fear or necessity. **Needs close supervision and constant encouragement.**
LI/LS

SKILLS — HIGH ... LOW

Skills Plus Interest

The Performance Matrix looks at the two factors most essential to high performance; interest and skills. Notice that this matrix does not say "interests", but rather "interest."

Interests can cover a lot of things. They can be mild interests or strong ones, work related or not. Most people have many interests; movies, music, sports, reading, nature, animals, people, and a whole array of other things. They are not necessarily motivated enough by each of the things they find interesting to learn the skills necessary to do a good job at them however.

"Interest," on the other hand implies a more singular involvement. We maintain the kind of interest implied in the singular only insofar as the interest continues to meet our dominant needs and bring us satisfaction. This can be seen in everything from relationships, to play, to the work we do.

We tend to maintain associations with people who continue to meet our needs and add to our sense of satisfaction, for instance, and to avoid or end relationships with people who don't. We also work and play at things that continue to meet our needs and add to our sense of satisfaction.

If interest is lacking, even things considered recreational are not pursued. Almost everyone can name leisure activities they have tried and decided were not enjoyable enough to continue doing. Snow skiing is one of those things for me. Many people love snow skiing and will head to the slopes every chance they get. Not me. I tried it and, while it was alright, I didn't especially enjoy the effort necessary to get suited up for skiing and I don't enjoy the cold. I much prefer a warm, sunny beach. Neither the actions nor the environment connected to skiing interest me, so I am not motivated to do it.

If loss of interest causes us to disengage from *play*, imagine what happens when we lose interest in the work we are doing or the environment in which we do the work.

This happens in organizations all the time and, when it does, rather than trying to discover why interest has diminished and find ways to reengage disinterested employees, most organizations start looking for another training program to put them through; and it never works. Without interest, the employee is just going through the prescribed motions and the appalling statistics on the effectiveness of typically applied training readily attests to this fact.

Star Performers

Take a look at the matrix. The star performer in the upper left-hand section has the ideal combination of high interest and high skills. This ideal combination only occurs when the developed skills are complementary to naturally preferred abilities, when job-related tasks complement both nature and training, and when leadership and the environment are also a fit.

The Proficiency Trap and Burnout

Burnout increases as interest decreases. Any adult of normal intelligence can learn skills over a relatively wide range and, once the skills are learned sufficiently well, the individual will test as having strength around that learned process. But strengths and motivators are two very different things.

I have training in accounting and am good at crunching numbers, but I have no interest in it so am not motivated to perform that job. If I had to, I could perform the function and do it well for awhile. But it wouldn't take long for me to get to Burnout (high skills/low interest) and lose momentum.

I love training and development and creating products that quickly move people to high levels of effectiveness. I never get tired of seeing leaders step into their real power and teams make game-changing leaps forward in mere hours.

Gina is exceptional at managing details. She is an excellent proof-reader and editor. These skills always show up on tests, such as the Gallop Strengths Finder, as strengths for her, but she has very little interest in doing them for extended periods of time.

Julie is good at conducting skills based training workshops and at one point in her career rather enjoyed it. She could certainly still conduct them and do a good job if she had to, but after she began coaching leaders she found that she much preferred coaching. Having become proficient at a more enjoyable skill set, going back to the previous and less preferred one would be unrewarding and draining.

Glen is good at creating training programs, having developed some 80 different ones throughout his career. He is highly capable of conducting needs analyses, designing programs, developing instructor manuals and participant workbooks, and constructing evaluations. Yet these don't hold his interest for long. His real interest is instruction; getting up in front of a room full of people and facilitating a training class.

Many people are proficient at things for which they have no passion. I call this the proficiency trap, and people get caught in it all the time. There are two reasons why:

1. People tend to get reinforced for what they do well. Since we are all motivated to move away from pain and toward pleasure, and the unconscious mind interprets reinforcement as pleasure, it is a powerful motivator even when the activity is not personally pleasurable. Psychological pleasure (compliments and acceptance) is just as motivating as physical or mental pleasure, but it is externally driven and hard to sustain.

2. Learning goes from unconscious incompetence (we don't know that we don't know) to unconscious competence (we know how to do something well enough that we don't have to think about it anymore). Both unconscious incompetence and unconscious competence are comfortable states so we seek to maintain them. The two learning stages in between—conscious incompetence (we know that we don't know) and conscious competence (we are not good enough at it not to have to think our way through it)—are uncomfortable, so we avoid those. On one end of the learning curve is ignorant bliss (unconscious incompetence) and on the other end is blissful proficiency. Learning a new skill takes us outside our comfort zone so we just keep doing what we already know how to do until the discomfort of doing that exceeds the discomfort of learning a new skill.

In both cases, we get caught in the proficiency trap because of our need to move away from pain and toward pleasure. Over the long term everyone is motivated by what naturally interests them, not by what they are capable of doing. It's just easier to keep doing what we know how to do and easier to get hired for that.

Most employers don't even bother to look for what a job candidate is interested in. They only want to know what the candidate can *do*. Yet, when employees' capabilities are not aligned with sustainable interest (natural abilities enhanced by complementary learned skills) and coupled with the right leadership and environment, the individual will inevitably burn out at some point. When they do, the typical response from an employer is to try to make the employee more capable when the solution is to make them more *interested*.

Going back to the matrix, notice that Star Performers and High Potentials are on the left (high interest) side. Also notice that the employee at or approaching burnout has high skills, but low interest. It is not uncommon for employees to come into an organization as Star Performers and move to Burnout because the nature of the job, the environment and/or leadership proves non-complementary. As organizational coaches and consultants, we have seen this occur many times.

There are three reasons why burnout occurs:

1. The job is not a good match and is unsatisfying

2. Leadership is ineffective

3. The environment is unhealthy

High Potentials

High potentials are people who have high interest in a particular arena, but insufficient training and low skills. It is not uncommon for organizations to assume that people who are effective in one position will be effective in another, but what makes a high potential is interest not skills. While a good work ethic and past performance is a good predictor of future performance, it does not follow that the performance will carry over into another type of job, another environment, or another type of leadership.

It is *not* always possible to take people who are high performers in one area and cross train them into another position and have them excel in the new position. A common example of this is moving a star salesperson or the best technician into a management position where more often than not they soon begin to flounder. They were stars in the original position because that position brought all the right elements together. They flounder as managers because the management position does not.

Except in the case of complex skills like medicine or engineering, it is always easier to create a Star Performer from someone who has the interest, but no skills, than from someone with the skills, but no interest. In fact, it is not possible to create a Star Performer where there is insufficient interest unless the factors that prevent interest are eliminated.

Strugglers

Organizations tend to look at employees that fit into the Struggler quadrant and assume the only thing they can or should do with these employees is get rid of them. That is not always the case. If the interest of such employees can be sparked, they can be moved from Struggler to High Potential, then all that is necessary is to provide them with the right training, which, in their case, *will* have an effect because the employee will be interested in learning. As interested employees gain the necessary skills, they begin moving up the scale toward Star Performer.

Rarely is training alone the catalyst for awakening disengaged employees. Individual and group coaching tend to be much more effective because coaches have more time to assess the individual and organizational dynamics and adjust their approach to whatever is needed. A good coach takes the time to discover employee interest and get them engaged before the learning process begins. But even here, organizations won't get the long term results they are hoping for until leaders get actively involved in creating a healthy culture and developing great leaders to sustain it.

Before any initiative will be effective, sleeping employees need to be awakened and reengaged. To do that, leaders must first find out what will interest them and find ways to provide it.

Unfortunately, typical OZ leaders have no interest in doing that. They argue that employees, and especially managers, just need to follow the rules and do what is expected of them. It's a catch-22 because to effectively do what is expected of them, employees must be engaged and to be engaged they have to be interested.

Frustrated Leaders

Because organizations are focused on the wrong part of the formula (skills rather than interest), managers are often at a complete loss as to how to improve performance. They keep prodding and training, but their employees remain disengaged. Many managers report with great frustration that, without the cooperation of top management, all their efforts are about as effective as butting their heads against a brick wall, and they are right.

Like the aircraft worker, most employees really do want to do a good job. They almost always come in the door with great hopes and expectations, and it usually takes a lot to cause them to shut down. The Poppy Effect typically sets in when disconnected leaders keep pushing employees to perform without giving them what they need to stay engaged.

I once went into an organization as a consultant/coach to the heads of several departments. In every department I heard horror stories about how the company's disconnected and completely out of touch CEO was wreaking havoc and preventing progress.

The team leaders in the product development division reported that they were extremely frustrated because, just the week before, they had met with the CEO and he had finally conceded that the project they had been working on for more than two years needed to be scrapped.

The engineers had known almost from day one that the project would not fly and they had collectively and individually informed the CEO of that fact in an effort to redirect it toward a successful outcome. They had presented a workable plan that would have resulted in a functional product, brought it to market faster and saved the company a lot of money, but the executive had discounted their expertise, ignored their advice and insisted that they pursue things his way no matter what they, as product development experts, suggested.

By the time the project got scrapped they had wasted more than just the two years, they had wasted untold resources. And, in spite of all they had done to prevent the losses, when the CEO finally decided to scrap the project, he actually accused the team of sabotaging the project to prove that they were right. When they protested the accusation of sabotage, the CEO recanted, but stated he believed the project failed because the team had not tried hard enough.

Were these engineers disengaged? Not completely, but without intervention they soon would have been. They were still feeling and expressing anger, disappointment and frustration over the time and resources that had been wasted, and these are not emotions that come from completely disengaged employees.

Completely disengaged employees don't even bother to express their anger anymore. Any passion they might have had for making a contribution to the company is gone and they no longer care whether the company is wasting time and resources. All they want to do is put in their time, collect their paycheck and sleepwalk through the day until it's time to go home.

While rules and procedures are necessary and even desirable to maintain structure and order, they need to serve the people as well as the organization. If they don't, they destroy initiative and kill any interest employees may have had in the job, the company, and the company's goals. Once the Poppy Effect takes over, any possibility of having an organization filled with high performing employees becomes little more than a distant dream.

CHAPTER TEN
The Wizard That Wasn't

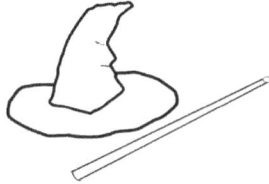

The heads of OZ corporations are masters at hiding from scrutiny. They surround themselves with layers of protection and avoid getting involved in anything that might expose their vulnerabilities. They are usually so far removed from the workforce that the only evidence many employees have that a leader even exists is circular evidence, and the Wizard wants to keep it that way.

In *The Wizard of Oz* film, Dorothy and her companions head off to Emerald City singing "If ever-oh-ever a wiz there was, the Wizard of Oz is one because; because... because... because... because... because of the wonderful things he does."

It doesn't matter that they have never personally seen any of the wonderful things the wizard supposedly does. His remoteness and the fact that he occupies the castle convince them that he surely must be able to do wonderful things. Why? Well... just because. It's a great illusion and the only way to sustain an illusion is to make sure lots of things stay hidden and the Wizard is well aware of this fact.

Those who buy into OZ organizational rules assume the Wizard can only be accessed by traveling the Yellow Brick Road; that is by following the rules, playing the game well and proving oneself worthy to arrive at the top of the corporate ladder. They think that if they can just get to that high place, they will surely be graced by the mighty leader, whom no ordinary person has ever really seen, but who everyone is sure is the one with the power to give them what they want.

Like Dorothy and her companions, many people travel that long road and finally arrive at the land of promised opportunity only to be disappointed when they are told, "No one can see the great OZ."

When someone is bold enough to ask, as Dorothy did, "Then how do you know there is one?" The troops respond, not with logic or proof, but with pomp and ceremony and pretty words designed to distract the inquirer from the facts, perpetuate the tradition, and maintain the Wizard's cover.

If the troops do their job sufficiently well, they are able to protect the Wizard and the seeker never discovers what's behind the curtain. The problem is, not only are the people unable to access the Wizard, the Wizard is also unable to access the people. As long as he is walled away and protected by pomp and ceremony and rhetoric, he is as clueless about what is happening among the people as they are about what's happening behind the curtain.

The world is changing and those changes are about to directly and significantly affect the organization that maintains the Wizard's lifestyle. The Wizard doesn't know this and neither does the organization that supports him any more than they know that the rules, roles, and policies they have relied on for years no longer work.

They don't yet know that the two generations about to take over the workforce are less organizationally focused than any generations since the pilgrims and more focused on aligning with their own personal values than any generations in history. Such news fills newspapers and the magazines the Wizard reads, but instead of looking at the organization and how it can successfully adjust to the new reality, the Wizard keeps busy trying to concoct some great new formula that will change the workforce.

Though it will never work and the Wizard only has a dozen or so years to figure that out, he still keeps trying because he is too disconnected to know that this is no mere trend. Neither can he see or comprehend that the focus on human values will ultimately be a good thing that can actually help organizations achieve their goals faster, easier and better, at least for the organizations that are able to bridge the gap between the way things used to be and the way they are now. There will be a lot of growing pains in the process but managers will be able to save huge amounts of time and effort when they have self-directed employees empowered to perform.

The illustration on the next page provides a quick overview of generational values and may help to put the growing gap into better perspective. Looking at the differences in values and approach, it becomes clear that the exodus from OZ will continue. As Baby Boomers retire and are replaced by a Generation X and Millennial workforce the shift toward self-reliance and individual requirements for satisfaction will continue to expand. We firmly believe that organizations that continue to resist this growing trend will not survive.

	Traditionals 1922-1945	Baby Boomers 1946-1964	Generation X 1965-1980	Millennials 1981-2002
Work Ethic & Values	Work hard, respect authority, adhere to rules, duty first	Work efficiently, question authority, champion causes, seek personal fulfillment	self-reliance, self-guidance, free to do the job and leave when done	self-reliance, entrepreneurial, independent contractor mindset
Work is Seen As	An obligation to be taken seriously	An arena for learning, growth and financial security	A negotiable contract which can be honored or broken	A means to an end, no more important than other aspects of life
Leadership Style	Follow directives, command and control	Consensual, laissez-faire	Equilateral, extends right to question and challenge	Collaborative, personally and socially responsible
Motivators	Respect for experience and capabilities	Recognition, position, money, significance	Opportunity to contribute their way, flex time, few rules	Personally/socially meaningful work, work/life balance
Preferred Rewards	Security, money, benefits	Tangible rewards, promotions	Plenty of freedom and flexibility	Respect, participation in meaningful projects
Preferred Feedback	Acknowledgement of accomplishments	Acknowledgement of contribution/value	Fair and specific feedback on work	Information at the push of a button
Work & Family	Two different worlds, work must come first	Work to live, leaning toward work	Seeks to achieve work/life balance	Insists upon work/life balance

Generational Overview

The trend doesn't just impact corporations either. It affects every kind of organization. For example, studies of the United States armed forces reveal severe retention problems.

Highly skilled Generation X and Millennial junior officers and enlisted service personnel are leaving in droves. Higher paying civilian jobs are sometimes cited as the cause, but that is by no means the only reason the problem exists.

According to surveys and exit interviews, most military personnel are not leaving for financial reasons, but because they are not willing to deal with typical command and control military leadership styles and rules they don't agree with. As in other traditional organizations, the younger generations report that the older and more senior-ranking officers don't understand their needs or manage them properly.

Mobile Generations

Another factor driving the problem and widening the gap is that Generation X and Millennials don't tend to enter any workplace, including the military, planning on staying there throughout their career. They are unwilling to sacrifice their family and life for their job and are not opposed to exiting situations where such sacrifices continue to be the norm.

The values held by the younger generations are frequently characterized negatively by older generations and the older generations tend to react to them harshly. The result is that the younger generations do what their values dictate—they leave.

Values honed in the crucible of major life events in the early teen years are there to stay. These values are powerful motivators that drive behavior, thought and belief—and they do not change. They are more powerful motivators than socioeconomics, gender, ethnicity, race and education.

The inability of OZ organizations to adjust to the new work ethics and values continues to drive the tendency of the younger generations to abandon ship and go to work for smaller companies or start their own entrepreneurial ventures; a dynamic that is costing large, bureaucratic organizations billions of dollars every year—and may eventually cost them their existence.

Generation X and Millennials are not thrilled with corporate life to start with. They tend to distrust institutions in general and institutional leaders in specific. They deeply resent the assumptions of the older generations that they will eventually "grow up" and learn to value the same things the older generations value.

Clearly, their work ethics and values are different. The Wizards can see that and they complain about it quite loudly. That the new workforce is never going to adopt the values and work ethics of previous generations, seems to be a fact that Wizards don't want to accept, however. They continue to push their own agendas and to complain when the result continues to be a mass exodus. This is not going to change either. According to our research, a very large percentage of Generation X and Millennial workers working for Corporate America plans to leave corporate life as soon as possible and find or create options they believe will suit them better than any role they can imagine ever having in the typical corporate environment.

Gen Xer, Carolann, is a classic example of what is happening across the nation "I used to consider myself a corporate refugee," Carolann reported. "Although I consistently built enclaves in which people who worked with my groups could do their best work every day, play to their strengths and feel a sense of contribution, as their leader in a vacuum of real leadership I was left to battle those whose only agenda was their own self-promotion. As I rose through the ranks, more and more often I was asked to behave in ways that were antithetical to my values. Overworked and burnt out, I disengaged, which left me feeling drained, bored and powerless. My vivid epiphany, which is what I ended up naming my company, was that it doesn't have to be this way," Carolann explained.

"I wasn't playing a big enough game on a big enough field, and I saw no wisdom in spending one more day of my life in a company I didn't trust. So I started my own company. I wanted to use my gifts as a leader to empower others to live their passion and purpose, however they see fit; something Corporate America wouldn't let me do.

I love helping people find their 'what's next' and I am actively working to help them find that in places that they historically can't—like in Corporate America. I do this by teaching people to be the leaders of themselves—the kind of leaders that we've all been waiting for; to be people we want to follow because we trust them, because we know that they will do the right thing, because they will make the hard decisions. It is our job to create a culture in which innovative thinking and greatness, instead of mediocrity and mindlessness are the price of admission."

I know Carolann and know that she is a real powerhouse. Any organization would be fortunate to have her as an employee. Corporate America had her, and many thousands like her in their employ once and failed to see what they had. Organizations, as most are now structured, will never have Carolann again. She doesn't trust them. And once trust is gone, it's over for these generations.

Organizations are still full of highly capable workers that are regularly over-controlled, under-utilized and grossly mismanaged, and they are actively looking for a way out. And there are some really smart people, like Carolann, actively working at showing these "corporate refugees" how to get out of environments these generations find oppressive and "become leaders of themselves." This trend can be stemmed, but certainly not in the way organizations are trying to do it at present.

You Might Try Asking

Most organizations are going about trying to hold onto these bright, independent young workers in all the wrong ways. They try to push their own agendas off on them and often find themselves in a pickle as a result.

Even when leaders think they are doing something for the benefit of the employee, they often find themselves in trouble because they have made assumptions based on their own ethics and values rather than considering those of the employees. Employers could easily find out what will work just by asking and being open to the answers they get, but far too few ever bother.

One example of this assumptive approach is a top consulting firm whose leaders decided that life/work balance was what their employees needed so they set out to promote the company's position on leading a balanced life. They began pushing the idea to their young professionals as a reason to stay with the company and couldn't understand why the employees were not responding as expected.

What they didn't know, because they had not bothered to check, is that several of their top performers were young and single, and were not interested in "a balanced life" at that time. What they wanted was to work as hard as possible and make as much money as possible as quickly as possible. They wanted to gain experience, save up their money and create a life position that would allow more freedom in the future when they were no longer young and single.

The young professionals considered the pitch they were getting from leaders to be paternalistic, offensive, and of zero value to them. They were go-getters that were very annoyed at being asked to make personal sacrifices so others could leave work early and spend time with their families (Roberto 2008).

Making unilateral decisions on behalf of employees is a pretty common practice in OZ organizations. The Wizard and his cronies still don't realize that people today are far more enlightened and aware than those in the past. They don't want or need their leaders to decide what is good for them. They don't appreciate it. They don't trust people who make decisions based on blind assumptions either, and they sure don't trust anyone who stays hidden away in some ivory tower thinking he or she has all the answers.

One of the greatest factors separating OZ leaders from Visionary Leaders is trust, and there is a direct correlation between trust and the degree of transparency and accessibility a leader allows. If OZ leaders understood this, perhaps they would be more willing to step out of the shadows and into the light of day.

MBWA

Visionary Leaders are very accessible to their people. Jack Welch, the former head of General Electric, made the company very successful through a process coined "management by walking around" (MBWA) by a team of leaders at Hewlett-Packard. The style was popularized by Tom Peters and Robert Waterman in their book *In Search of Excellence* in 1982. The strength of MBWA lies in informal communication and in getting management out of the office and into the real world of work so they can discover, first-hand, what employees want and need to succeed.

OZ leaders often protest that MBWA is an old, tired and outdated idea. They claim that in the information age with communications zipping along at the speed of light, they don't need to bother. They make themselves available through e-mail, they say, and they insist that it is much more efficient.

Efficient perhaps, but is it effective? Based on dozens of studies, from the Gallup employee engagement study to generational needs studies, the answer is a resounding "no!" E-mail is not a leader's friend. It almost always leads to *less* connection, deeper distrust, ever more impenetrable silos, and less productivity and profits. E-mail has simply provided OZ leaders with another excuse for staying hidden behind the assumed security of the ever-drawn curtain.

Hiding behind a computer increases the distance between leaders, their employees, and their customers. With the greater distance and the justification for keeping it now attributable to the need to attend to all the e-mails and electronic reports, the focus on earnings tends to increase and the connection to people continues to erode.

In the information age, leaders have become less connected and more focused on quarterly earnings. In fact, shareholders now have more direct access to top executives than most employees. Shareholders also tend to be much bolder about asking for what they want and expect and, as always, the loudest voice is the one most often heard and heeded.

As shareholders push harder for healthier earnings, leaders push harder on managers to stay within a budget while at the same time increasing productivity. Managers, in turn, push supervisors to get more out of workers and workers, feeling unseen and unappreciated, rebel or disengage. This vicious cycle can hardly be called connecting even by the wildest stretch of the imagination.

For those who have not yet managed to peek behind the curtain, here's what you can expect to find when you do. No matter how much bravado a Wizard manages to muster, what keeps him (or her) hidden away is fear and insecurity. Truly confident people rarely feel a need to separate themselves from others or to hide away and surround themselves with gatekeepers.

Real Leaders

Some of the most effective leaders on the planet are the most highly accessible. Herb Kelleher of Southwest Airlines is a good example. Kelleher grew Southwest Airlines from a small Texas-only commuter airline to the gold standard in national airline carriers.

Southwest Airlines became so successful and effective that the company has been studied by every other carrier and even by management schools all across the nation. Southwest Airlines has become the company to emulate. Why? Because Southwest Airlines makes *more profits* than other airlines. Even during the great recession, Southwest Airlines managed to turn a profit, and other companies want to know how.

When Kelleher was the active head of the organization he developed a reputation for showing up in the most unexpected places playfully interacting with his employees. There are thousands of stories told by former and current employees of his endearing way of interacting with them. Although other airlines studied and copied Kelleher's processes, procedures and systems, they have still failed to meet with his success.

Someone once asked Kelleher if he was concerned that other airlines were copying his business strategies and systems and he answered "Not in the least." When asked why, he replied that his success was not in his systems, but in his people, which his competitors did not have and did not know how to create. The reality is that Kelleher had great people because of his leadership style. He encouraged them to be great. He expected it. And, as most people are prone to do, his employees met expectations. Typical of Visionary Leaders, Kelleher gave all the credit to his people, but it all started with him.

He was right not to worry about his competitors and he knew it. He knew that any organization focused on strategies and systems would never have the advantage Southwest Airlines had because they were focused on the wrong things.

To Leave a Legacy You Must Live a Legacy

Some OZ leaders are so focused on leaving a legacy that they fail to live a legacy as Herb Kelleher has done. In successful organizations, legacies begin and end with the results that were realized on that particular leader's watch. And exceptional results are always a product of exceptional people who are inspired and then set free to excel.

In OZ organizations people are treated as a commodity, not as bundles of potential. They are even referred to as "human capital" in many such organizations. How much more commoditized can you get?

On average, people tend to rise to whatever level of excellence is expected of them, but the expectations must be genuine and legitimate. A disconnected leader cannot possibly have legitimate expectations because they don't see or appreciate their employees in any real sense. When employees sense this, they are not very motivated to perform.

OZ leaders tend to point to the low performance levels of their employees as proof that they are right to keep cracking the whip and making demands. What they don't realize is that when they look at unmotivated employees, they are looking at the *effect* of their leadership, not at the cause of the problem. To see the *cause*, they will need a mirror.

Not all leaders in OZ organizations are Wizards intent only on protecting their position. Some keep themselves separated from their people not because they care more about keeping their ego and position in tact than about their people, but because they don't know how to get past all the OZ rules and roles, past all the pomp and ceremony, past the politics and power plays, past what so many people expect them to be.

An example of leaders who are willing to do what is necessary when they have the right tools is a client of Glen's, a financial institution with all kinds of rules and regulations. Glen was called in because the company was steadily losing customers and didn't know why or what to do about it. In reviewing the organization, Glen suggested that the organizational culture needed to be significantly altered and offered a way to do that. The leaders were open to trying it.

At the time customer service employees were individual contributors with a unique set of job duties that each had been performing for 5 to 15 years depending on the length of their employment. The plan was to form intact workgroups of 5-7 employees, where each team had a specific set of customers. The goal was to build cohesive teams that would improve customer service, increase customer satisfaction and retention, regain old customers and attract new ones.

Glen performed individual and focus group interviews, customized a training program, conducted training to build team cohesiveness, and oversaw the cross-training processes to ensure that all teams were able to perform the job functions specific to their team.

The results were phenomenal; error rates dropped by 50%, turnover went from 35% to .02%, customer satisfaction rates increased significantly, current customers were retained and new ones added, and the company saved over $400K in the first year.

How did it happen? Senior management bought in and did their part. They informed all employees of the problem and the proposed solution and solicited their active involvement in achieving the goal. The employees rose to the occasion, as involved employees tend to do, and agreed to help.

As they began operating in teams and understood that the whole team failed if one member failed, they became invested in helping each other succeed. Instead of sitting idly when there was slack time as they had done as individual contributors, they now got up and voluntarily helped their teammates. They also began to collectively solve error problems and handle customers differently.

Rather than getting any one of hundreds of people in a call center, the customer was now routed to "their team." Team members came to know their customers and their situations so were better able to help them. This minimized frustrations for both the customers and the team members and in just a few months healthy relationships were developing between the teams and their customers.

Behind the Curtain

Many leaders in OZ organizations are much like the man behind the curtain in the story. The real man was just an ordinary guy from Nebraska who landed in Oz and found himself thrown into a position of praise and expected leadership.

He had learned a few tricks as a stage magician, which he used to create an illusion that would meet the expectations of the people who looked up to him. By surrounding himself with props and remaining inaccessible he was able to appear to be as great and powerful as the people expected him to be. Once he had created the illusion he didn't know how to step away from it and be authentic.

Just as the wizard in the story was actually relieved when he was finally exposed and forced to tell his truth, so too are many leaders in OZ organizations. And, given the tools and resources to get back to their authentic roots, many are delighted to take that journey back home.

Many leaders who appear to be OZites simply lack the tools to affect the positive change they desire. They keep themselves separated out of frustration or fear and, while they certainly need to make some major changes, they are not the ones that will bring an organization down.

The ones that are, and will continue to be, real problems are the ones that love the role of Wizard and can't get past their own egos. Pseudo-Wizards are open to learning so can be redeemed. It's the egotists that need to be dethroned.

As we continue to explore Wizards and the negative effect they have on the workforce, it will be useful to remember that not all leaders who appear to be Wizards really are. You can know the difference by evaluating the lengths to which they will go to protect their ego.

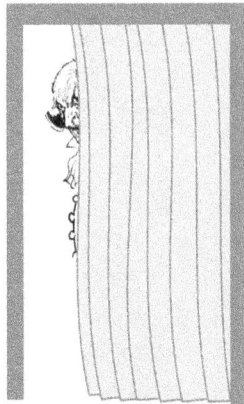

Do not arouse the wrath of the great and powerful Oz!
The Wizard from *The Wizard of OZ*

CHAPTER ELEVEN
Just Do One More Thing

When Dorothy and her companions finally manage to get an audience with the wizard, she is surprised and confused that he is unwilling to grant the requests they have traveled so far to make. After all, Glinda the Good Witch, a source Dorothy considered trustworthy, assured her that if she could just get to the Emerald City, the Great Oz would help her. She conveyed that information to her companions based on what seemed to be credible information and now it appears she was misinformed.

How many times have employees of OZ organizations had that experience? They are told to follow the rules, stay on the path, go the distance, and the prize will be theirs. As was the case with Glinda, those giving that advice often believe they are telling the truth so convey the message very convincingly.

It is not uncommon for trusting employees, based on what seemed like credible advice, to go the distance only to have the Wizard throw out yet another challenge when they finally arrive at his door.

In the story of Oz, the wizard, to cover his ineptness, sets Dorothy and her companions off on a task that he is certain they cannot accomplish. The wizard apparently believes that when they fail and he doesn't grant them their wishes, they will think it is their own fault and will never suspect that the wizard has no power to grant their wishes in the first place.

All the poor, unsuspecting foursome will know is that they failed. And, having failed, they won't think they deserve the reward and will go away. It's a pretty effective way to maintain the illusion of great and powerful.

The way this often happens in OZ organizations is through the practice of "rewarding" the best employees for all their hard work and dedication by giving them *more* work to do and convincing them that taking on the added responsibility will make them look good to the people at the top.

In the beginning, the story sounds plausible and the extra responsibility appears to be a vote of confidence. So taking on additional work can actually seem like a reward, or at least the promise of one, and the employee enthusiastically takes it on.

Eventually the extra load becomes a burden, especially when the promised rewards don't materialize. As the employee's enthusiasm and energy levels drop, their interest in pleasing management lessens and the employee begins the downward spiral toward burnout.

As the employee's interest in taking on more work begins to wane, OZ strategies change. Now, rather than telling the hard working employee how valuable he or she is, the OZ leader begins to overtly or covertly convey disappointment. It doesn't take much of that for the employee's interest to vanish altogether and what was once a Star Performer becomes an angry, disengaged employee.

In a traditional workforce, employees put up with this kind of "reward" because traditional employees were taught that hard work is part of the job. It was a badge of honor. Traditional workers were also taught to respect leadership and not challenge authority, so they just dealt with feeling over-worked and burned out.

Today's generations do not live or work by those rules. They believe they have basic rights which include appropriate rewards for work well done. They are more willing to question authority and challenge assumptions that don't fit their model and more willing to ask for what they think they deserve.

Many Generation X and the Millennials grew up in homes where open discussions with their parents were the norm. They were encouraged to make their own choices and to understand and honor their own values. Like Dorothy, today's generations want to know "Why can't you just give us what we want?"

The X and Millennial generations are filled with feisty people who know what they want and are not afraid to ask for what they think they are worth. They refuse to blindly follow orders, especially if the orders go against their values or compromise their sense of self, so cannot be easily manipulated into something they don't want to do.

A classic example of this is Susan, the Director of Engineering for an international organization. She has been with her company for twelve years, and is an exceptional employee. Her boss wants to move her into a VP position, and he's giving her extra duties to prepare her for it.

The problem is that Susan does not want the job! She has two small children and simply does not want the lifestyle that the position would require. Her boss continues to encourage her to get on track for the VP role, and Susan keeps standing her ground. As this unwelcome dance continues, Susan's stress level increases and her effectiveness decreases.

Even though the position her boss wants her in would pay more money, money is not what Susan values most. She values time with her family. So although she likes her current job, she does not believe her boss will let up and is actively looking for another position where she will be valued for what she contributes and not pushed into something she does not want.

Susan is performing her job well as she always has, but she is focused on a different prize and is growing weary of her disconnected boss's refusal to see it. If he would stop pushing, Susan would continue to do an exceptional job in her current role and be happy to do it. But, he won't. He will keep pushing, certain he is right, until he loses a highly valuable employee.

Don't Ask, Don't Tell

In 1993 the federal government mandated a "Don't ask—Don't tell" policy for the military in regards to sexual orientation. The stated reason for this policy was to prevent "an unacceptable risk to the high standards of morale, good order and discipline, and unit cohesion that are the essence of military capabilities."

This is the classic approach of bureaucracies and other OZ organizations. "Don't ask—Don't tell" kept up the façade of civility and prevented communication on any meaningful level. All this kind of initiative does is create a situation in which silos develop between departments, and between leaders and their employees. It encourages dishonesty, deception and concealment, none of which could be considered elements for "team cohesion" by any stretch of the imagination.

Teams require communication to have any semblance of cohesion, but when it has been demonstrated that honesty has a price, employees are not too inclined to speak their mind or tell the truth.

When communications break down, a breakdown in employee morale and engagement are not far behind; not exactly a desirable result in the military, or in any other organization.

Secrecy is never the answer. Transparency, honesty, and open communication are key elements to building trust and trust is a critical element for team cohesion. Only in OZ would anyone assume otherwise.

Silos of Silence

In siloed organizations it is not uncommon for a manager to throw out an idea and ask for feedback, only to have employees feed back what they believe the manager wants to hear. The leaders are then left with the illusion that communication has occurred and employees are in agreement with their position. It is also not uncommon for the project everyone "agreed" was a good idea to fail to gain any momentum.

Honest feedback is scarce in organizations where silos of silence exist and they are very common in OZ organizations because OZ leaders tend to believe that the best way to lead is to stay separated from the workers except to issue orders or maybe pit one employee against another to foster competition. They erroneously believe that more gets done through competition than through cooperation, so they encourage competition.

Leaders who understand and promote the value of cooperation don't fare too well in OZ organizations. In fact, they are routinely devalued by overly competitive OZ leaders and pushed to be more competitive.

While conducting a soft 360 interview for Dave, one of Julie's clients, Julie interviewed the divisional CEO. The feedback from the CEO was that Dave "didn't have a leadership bone in his body." That was not the feedback she got from Dave's employees.

They reported that he was a great leader who was well liked and trusted by them. In fact, the general consensus was that they would "walk through fire for him". Clearly, the CEO was not able to see what Dave's people saw. He had his own view of what a leader should look like and that was all that mattered.

Never mind that Dave's gentle style had built employee loyalty and created a level of performance uncommon in a dysfunctional environment. He wasn't ruling with an iron fist so something had to change. Something did. Dave eventually left and most of his team followed.

There is no greater leader than one that people will happily follow, but OZ leaders don't see it that way. They have an image of what leaders should look like and the image is someone just like them; tough, aggressive, opinionated, judgmental, demanding, highly competitive and distanced from the "little people".

Prodding for Performance is a Poor Practice

OZ leaders are always prodding the kinder, gentler leaders to get tougher, but that runs contrary to this type of leader's nature. So the prodding only results in increased stress, not better management. Without all the stress inducing prodding, these gentle, caring souls make exceptional middle managers. Even with the stress, many of them tend to get better results from their people because they tend to protect their employees from the Wizard's ego and ire, absorbing all the pressure themselves and enduring the stress for the sake of their people.

Such leaders stay in OZ organizations primarily to protect their employees, but the toll on them is a very heavy one. The trend toward staying to protect their team is shifting though. Gen X and Millennial leaders are far more prone to defying the leader covertly and many leave, taking their team with them.

An example of covert defiance is a very effective female executive who opted to stay in the organization she worked for until she had perfected her plan for leaving. She explained her strategy as much like playing a game of chess with the OZ CEO. She carefully thought out her moves to ensure that the CEO was never able to checkmate her, which in her opinion, was clearly his intent. She played the game as much to protect her people and to take a stand for them as she did to protect her own position. Her thought was that, at the end of the day, she would be judged by how well she led her people and, other than keeping the Wizard at bay, that is what she stayed focused upon.

This leader still keeps her strategies close to the vest because she knows that to reveal anything to the OZ leader could compromise any advantage she might gain for herself and her people. She is direct enough to disagree with him, but only to an extent. She knows her opinions won't change the OZ leader's style, but stating them when it's important allows her to stay true to her own values.

"My way or the highway" is a very ineffective way of "leading". In fact, it isn't leadership at all. It is coercion. Yet many OZ leaders not only take this position, they push it off on those in leadership positions below them.

The big problem with this approach is that today's generations don't perform when coerced. They disengage. The harder they are pushed to perform without question or consideration, the more they disengage. This is not a battle OZ leaders can win, though they keep trying.

A Radical New Approach

Some OZ leaders are aware that their tactics are not working. What they don't yet seem to understand is that they will *never* work! The only way they can lead today's workforce effectively is to change their entire approach. That means stepping out from behind the curtain and genuinely connecting with the people in the organization. We have found that most are not able to do that without the help of a good coach.

Leaders and managers in OZ organizations tend to point to others as the source of the problem. They regularly complain that Generation X and Millennial employees have no work ethic or sense of loyalty, and that this is what is causing all the problems.

The fact is, these generations have plenty of work ethic and are fiercely loyal to organizations that support and value them, but they do not and will not tolerate those that do not.

To get a real look at today's workers and what they are capable of, look at Google, the world's largest search engine company, Facebook the leading social media site, and Starbucks, currently the world's largest chain of coffee houses. Also look a Zappos, the online shoes and clothing company whose mission statement is to "deliver happiness" to employees, customers, vendors, everyone. These organizations understand today's generations because they belong to them.

Each of these companies has very loyal employees who are dedicated to doing a good job. With the help of a team of dedicated employees, most of whom are Generation X and Millennials, these organizations have gone from mere ideas to billion dollar organizations in just a few short years. I don't know of a single OZ organization that has ever experienced such meteoric results.

Research indicates that winning the prize (the promotion or the raise) is not the primary motivator for today's generations. They want involvement. They want communication. They want meaningful connections and to do meaningful work. They want to live true to their values and they are unwilling to compromise them for an external, and in their view temporary, reward.

Today's generations are socially conscious people who want to make a real difference, and blindly following orders goes completely against their grain. That's why what used to work does not work now and will never work again. To think it will is delusional.

The younger generations are never going to "shape up" and start acting like Traditionals the way Baby Boomers eventually did. Baby Boomers complied because they were shaped by traditional parents. That was not the case for most Gen Xers and Millennials.

Order in a Chaotic World

By the time they were in their early teens, Gen Xers decided that government and big businesses could not be trusted and they decided to stay as distant and disengaged from these institutions as possible.

Millennials grew up hearing from the Xers that organizations and institutions were not to be trusted and that the future could not be counted upon to yield anything of value. The Millennials saw evidence that this was true, but rather than merely disengage, they decided to create their own future.

We now have two generations of people that, for different reasons, are not intimidated by the fear tactics that worked with past generations, so the tactics used by OZ organization in the past do not, and will not, work with today's generations.

The typical view of the workplace is aptly described by Margaret Wheatley, author of *Leadership and the New Science: Discovering Order in a Chaotic World*. She says, "I sit in a room without windows, participating in a ritual etched into twentieth-century tribal memory. I have been here thousands of times before, literally. I am in a meeting, trying to solve a problem. Using whatever analytic tool somebody has just read about or been taught at their most recent training experience, we are trying to come to grips with a difficult situation. Perhaps it is poor employee morale or productivity. Or production schedules. Or the redesign of a function. The topic doesn't matter. What matters is how familiar and terrible our process is for coming to terms with the complaint. The room is adrift in flip chart paper—clouds of lists, issues, schedules, plans, accountabilities—crudely taped to the wall. They crack and rustle, fall loose, and, finally, are pulled off the walls, tightly rolled, and transported to some innocent secretary, who will litter the floor around her desk so that, peering down from her keyboard, she can transcribe them to tidy sheets, which she will mail to us. They will appear on our desks days or weeks later, faint specters of commitments and plans, devoid of even the little energy and clarity that sent the original clouds—poof!—up onto the wall. They will drift into our day planners and onto individual 'to do' lists; lists already fogged with confusion and inertia. Whether they get 'done' or not, they will not solve the problem. I am weary of the lists we make, the time projections we spin out, the breaking apart and putting back together of problems. It just does not work" (Wheatley 2009).

This is the way so many employees describe their work experience. What is missing here? The care and feeding of the human heart and soul; some semblance of authentic humanity. And it is the absence of these that send today's generations in search of a new company to call home every year or so. It is why record numbers of them are starting their own companies and abandoning the "rat race". Their approach is a result of fundamental generational differences that are not going to change.

Fundamental Failure

It is failure to understand the fundamental generational differences, and the right of the younger generations to have them, or the refusal of the older generations to acknowledge and respect these differences that is creating many of the conflicts workgroups are experiencing today.

An example of the lack of understanding is a manufacturing plant where Glen once worked. The leaders in this company had been using the traditional method of a forced day off without pay for shop-floor hourly workers as a discipline measure. This method was not working for Gen X and Millennial employees. In fact, it had the exact opposite effect for these generations than for their Baby Boom co-workers.

After months of puzzling over this, one of the leaders finally decided to talk to employees to try to discover why. What they found was that, while Baby Boomers saw the action as a loss of income and were embarrassed at being forced to take time off, Gen X and Millennial workers saw the time off without pay as a mini-vacation and actually enjoyed it.

Since the identity of Baby Boomers was so closely tied to their job, they had a problem with being seen as a "bad" employee. That was not at all the case for the Gen X and Millennial workers.

After much discussion, the company changed the way they disciplined employees and started assigning extra work as a means of discipline. Even though the employees were paid for the extra time, extra work was seen as a form of punishment by all employees and disciplinary issues dropped.

Generational conflict often occurs in the workplace as a result of the refusal of the older generations to acknowledge the right of the younger generations to have different needs and values. Often this gap in understanding creates conflict where none need exist.

An example of this is a team of civilian employees working with the military. The organization had adopted a flex-time system that allowed employees to choose when they came to work and left as long as they put in their eight hours. Even though the flexibility was allowed, and even encouraged, major conflict developed between the generations in the areas of timeliness and attendance.

Baby Boomers still came to work early and left late, and interpreted not doing so as disrespectful and lacking consideration for the team. Gen Xers and Millennials considered their non-work activities to be just as important as work activities so they would show up on their own schedule, work diligently until their eight hours were up and then promptly leave.

The Baby Boomers on this team had high amounts of unused vacation time and were proud of that fact. The Gen Xers and Millennials used their vacation time as soon as they earned it, often taking three day weekends to spend extra time with their friends and families, and they were just as proud of that.

The Baby Boomers felt very resentful of the Gen Xers and Millennials and regularly criticized the "lack of commitment and work ethic" they thought the two younger generations exhibited. This resulted in frequent conflict within this group. Not until they understood the differences at a values level were the Baby Boomers able to allow the Gen Xers and Millennials to work within the system in their own way.

Generation X and Millennials don't really lack commitment or a work ethic, and, like previous generations, they will perform—and perform well—for the right reasons. They won't perform without question and the prize is not what it used to be, but like every generation before them, they perform beautifully under the right conditions. To get the most from today's workforce is going to require a whole new set of rules, however, and until organizations figure this out and adjust they will continue to experience conflict and chaos.

The fundamental failure is in understanding the power of values, which do not change for any generation. The unchanging values of Baby Boomers is what drove the addition of workout rooms, childcare facilities and cafeterias to many of today's workplaces. The incoming generations have as much right to the values they hold as any other generation has had. They know this too, and they are not about to settle for less.

"You cursed brat! Look what you've done! I'm melting!
Melting! Oh, what a world! What a world! Who would
have thought a good little girl like you could destroy my
beautiful wickedness?"

Wicked Witch of the West
From *The Wizard of OZ*

CHAPTER TWELVE
Conquering the Wicked Witch

The Wicked Witch represents leaders that are so frustrated, overworked, fearful, bitter or angry much of the time that they become negative and then push their negativity off on others. They feel powerless to change the organization's rules, influence leaders, or change the things that are making them miserable personally, so they use the power of their position to compensate.

They scream, yell, coerce, intimidate, push and cajole to whatever degree they deem necessary, and wield positional power with all the fury they can muster. This is to ensure that no one questions their power. They surround themselves with pawns, like the Flying Monkeys, to ensure that their fragile power is well protected.

Witches use criticism, sarcasm and fear to build up walls around themselves that are foreboding and seemingly insurmountable. The average person wouldn't dream of trying to breach them. The Witch is masterful at using other people's social conventions against them. Most people have been taught, for example, that it is improper or rude to make a scene. So Witches ensure that every time an employee does not meet their impossible standards, they are subjected to a scene where their mistake is loudly and visibly magnified.

The three major fears, ridicule, rejection and embarrassment, are the Witch's primary tools. These are often used in combination. When vague orders are not carried out in specific, the Witch uses all three fears to punish and communicate their power. If what the employee delivers does not meet the Witch's expectations, they will first ridicule: ("Why didn't you get it? Why are people so stupid?"). This is a combination of both aggressive and passive-aggressive behavior. The aggressive behavior is designed to maintain control. The passive-aggressive behavior is designed to keep the employee off balance.

Next, Witches go to rejection and they aren't just rejecting the work, they are rejecting the employee: "I can't believe you thought something like this would be acceptable!" Finally, the Witch uses embarrassment, making a scene in front of the employee's peers so they are aware that the boss finds this employee ineffective and inefficient.

The Witch's behaviors only work in the long term with employees that fear losing their jobs. The emerging problem for the Witch is that today's new workforce has no such fear. They don't play the guilt game and they are perfectly willing to look for another job if the current one isn't working.

Once the Baby Boom generation retires, it is questionable whether the Witch's tactics will continue to work. The fact that it doesn't work for a large percentage of Gen Xers and Millennials provides clues as to what other employees can do to derail the Witch. The formidable walls the Witch has built have proven no match for those brave souls on a mission or those who have no fear of losing their job.

These emboldened employees refuse to play the Witch's game. They seem to understand that the behaviors are really about the Witch's insecurities, and not about them. They are not embarrassed by their boss's inappropriate behaviors, and they don't generally take the rejection and ridicule personally. In their minds, it's just an opinion and they respond with, "Whatever!" An attitude that drives the Witch crazy!!

Conquering the Witch is actually a lot easier than it appears. The Witch is almost always insecure which makes her vulnerable to the employee that shows courage.

The scene from *The Wizard of Oz* where Dorothy was trying to protect the scarecrow (intellect) and accidentally threw water on the witch, is a metaphor for what has happened in the workplace of today. In defending their right to think for themselves, today's workforce has accidentally stumbled upon the way to overpower even the Witch.

The witch in the film protested the action with, "You cursed brat! Look what you've done! I'm melting! Melting! Oh, what a world! What a world! Who would have thought a good little girl like *you* could destroy my beautiful wickedness?" In this the witch has moved from tyrant to victim and is projecting her own bad behaviors onto Dorothy.

So it is with the organizational Witch. You either comply—and earn their ire and disrespect—or you fight back, in which case the Witch projects her bad behaviors onto you and deems you worthy of punishment. It is a no-win situation designed to ensure that the Witch's delicate ego stays protected and you remain powerless.

In the film, the witch melted when dowsed with water. In OZ organizations, essentially the same thing happens when the Witch is confronted by an individual that uses intellect to counter bad behaviors.

Past generations feared leadership so they could be intimidated and manipulated. Only the few who managed to conjure up enough courage to stand their ground were able to conquer the Witch, and they generally paid with their job.

Today's generations have an edge that previous generations didn't have. There is an old maxim in negotiations that states "he who is most willing to walk away has the most power." Most Gen Xers and Millennials are willing to walk away, which gives them a degree of power that previous generations did not have.

When an individual refuses to be intimidated or coerced by fear, those who use fear as a weapon have no power. And, since fear is the Witch's primary weapon, those who see it as a control tactic can easily conquer it.

Nick, a client of mine, was being routinely manipulated and intimidated by his Witch boss. The boss' agenda was to keep Nick in line and make him do his bidding, and it was working because Nick was committed to the company and to his team. He came looking for help because he didn't want to give up his job, but he didn't want to continue to have to deal with his difficult boss either. This was a dilemma to which he saw no solution.

The first thing that needed to happen was for Nick to recognize that he was being manipulated, and to recognize what manipulation looked like. He also needed to remove himself from the emotional entanglement created by his boss's knack for pushing hot buttons.

To provide Nick with a strategy that would remove him emotionally and help him recognize the manipulation, I instructed him to start keeping a log of each manipulative comment and behavior. Over the next month he logged 138 examples of manipulation from his boss.

Having logged the examples, I then asked him to put a tick mark by each manipulation as it was repeated so he would be aware of his boss's typical strategies. He found that twelve were repeated regularly. Before long Nick was able to recognize the frequently used manipulations by number so when the boss used one, he simply identified which one it was ("Okay, that's number 5") which took him out of the emotional loop and gave him a tremendous sense of control.

Soon he was able to ignore the manipulations and do his job in a way that supported his team and the company. Over time, Nick emerged as the team leader and the Witch boss was fired due to ineffectiveness. Nick was promoted into the management position and still excels there. This was one of those situations where, although the employee didn't aspire to the leadership position, he ended up with it because he chose to be an effective employee and helpful to his teammates in spite of dealing with an ineffective and manipulative boss. Nick got the promotion, not because he sought it out for himself, but because his teammates sought it for him.

Witches are often conquered by their own behaviors, especially when those they seek to intimidate stand their ground. Just as the vindictive actions of the witch in *The Wizard of Oz* led to her own demise, so too do the behaviors of the Witches in organizations.

It isn't usually OZ leaders that shut the Witch down either. It is usually the employees after they decide they have had enough and decide to do something about it. With the new workforce, that is more and more the approach. Our guess is that Witches the world over need to get prepared to be doused.

CHAPTER THIRTEEN
Claiming the Reward

When Dorothy and her companions were assigned the task of bringing back the witch's broom, they fully expected to receive the rewards they were promised upon delivery. What they got instead was more stalling. The wizard demanded that they "come back tomorrow." When Dorothy protested, the wizard bellowed, "You ungrateful creatures! Think yourselves lucky that I'm giving you audience tomorrow instead of *twenty years* from now!"

Delay tactics are not uncommon when OZ leaders promise things they either don't know how to deliver or have no intention of delivering. And, if the delay tactic doesn't work, intimidation usually does. Intimidation is a favorite tactic of OZ leaders and they can defer things for a very long time using that one tactic.

Like the wizard in the story, OZ leaders have discovered that most of the people in their employ can be intimidated into submission. All they have to do is keep escalating the aggression until employees become sufficiently afraid of losing their job if they persist.

In the past, employees rarely stood their ground unless they had come to the end of their rope and believed they had nothing left to lose. Not so with the newer generations. The problem OZ leaders are facing today is the fact that so many employees walk in the door with a "nothing-to-lose" attitude. Gen X and Millennials don't believe that they can count on anyone but themselves to get their outcomes, so they are ready and willing to challenge leadership to get what they believe they deserve.

When OZ leaders make promises that they are not able to fulfill, their ego typically won't allow them to admit it. To cover that fact, they throw up smoke screens and diversions, which are usually very effective at keeping everyone in the dark, including the leaders themselves.

Because they are disconnected from their people and the wants and needs of the people, they think all they need to do to keep employees satisfied and engaged is to hand out an occasional plaque or trophy that employees can sit on a shelf, or give them some fancy, but meaningless title. OZ Leaders generally have no idea what employees really want in exchange for their efforts and they can't bring themselves to ask. They would rather make assumptions than make themselves appear less than all knowing and all powerful, and the assumptions are often wrong.

Dorothy and her companions had no use for the broom. It was just a means to achieving their goals. The wizard never really wanted the broom either. For him it was just a means of deferring the inevitable and distracting the group from the fact that he could not give them what they wanted. To maintain his precarious position, he couldn't possibly admit that he was incapable of producing something an underling had the audacity to ask for.

Today's leaders need to get used to audacity though because the new workforce has plenty of it. Like Dorothy, they will do the job and deliver what the boss requests, but they are very clear that what they are doing is just a means to an end and they know what they want in return. Unlike previous generations, they don't silently accept alternate rewards. They speak out. They rebel. And, if that doesn't work, they walk out the door and don't come back.

A few unwelcome "rewards" employees in client organizations have reported receiving are:

- More work to do with no increase in pay or power

- Insincere compliments designed to induce more work

- Having territory and commissions reduced in response to strong sales

- A title with no authority or pay increase

- Token trophies and meaningless "incentives" based on the recommendations of the vendors that sell such items

All of these are ultimately *demotivators*. When top performers discover that good work is rewarded by more work and more responsibility rather than meaningful rewards, they soon stop performing so well.

When the best sales people are penalized for outperforming their peers by having their territory or commissions reduced, they lose the desire to make money for that organization and start looking for another one that will fairly reward their efforts.

When high performing employees get laid off with no consideration for what they have contributed, not only does the company lose good employees, but the remaining employees lose heart. "If really good employees have such little value," the remaining employees reason, "I don't stand a chance here."

OZ leaders tend to make poor judgment calls in developing strategies, dealing with crises and especially in leading people. They don't get the best from their people because they don't know what their people want or need. And, since they are not in the loop, they don't know what they don't know.

For example, the sales staff of a client company was given a quota which none of them ever managed to meet. In searching for the cause, I began with confidential interviews in which several salespeople informed me that meeting the company quota meant the quota would be increased by 10% the following year.

One of the salespeople had run projections over a four year period and realized that he would have to be doing 46% better in four years if he met quotas. He had shared this information with the other salespeople and they had all agreed that 10% per year and 46% in 4 years was an unreasonable expectation. Several of the salespeople stated that they had tried on various occasions to convey this to the CEO and on each occasion they were dismissed as "whiners". In time, the salespeople decided that they could not talk to leadership about their concerns so they stopped trying.

The annual quota was raised 2% when quotas were not met. The salespeople believed 2% was a more realistic increase so they collectively decided that they should not meet the quota. If no one met or exceeded the quota, they reasoned, the boss would have to assume it was the marketplace or some other outside factor and no one would be singled out and picked on—and the reasonable 2% would keep them growing at an acceptable rate.

By staying just under the quota, the salespeople still made a decent living and while they were not all content with that arrangement, they all felt it beat the alternative. Each of the salespeople had been with the company for more than three years and all were working as a team—but for one another—not for the company.

Within two days I had the solution to the problem because I asked the right questions and listened to those who had the answers. Something the CEO who hired me could have easily done. In asking the salespeople why they didn't meet their quotas and hearing about the 10% increase rule, I then asked the question no one else had bothered to ask, "What percentage of increase do you think would be fair to the company and doable for you?"

The answers ranged from 2% to 5%. I then brought the sales staff together and asked them to settle on a specific percentage and, in deciding, to consider their capabilities. When people consider their capabilities, they rarely under-estimate themselves so I expected they would come back with 5% and that's exactly what they did. That was more than twice what they had been maintaining, but they had been purposely holding back.

If the company agreed to the 5%, they told me, they were willing to work harder and smarter to meet the quota. In checking with each individually, every one of them believed they could reach the quota and each committed to genuinely try.

This was a problem that would be easy to solve with the cooperation of leadership, but based on the feedback from the sales staff, I wasn't sure I would get it. I counted on the fact that there was a clear hierarchy in this organization, which employees could not breach but which I, as an outside consultant paid to find solutions, might bypass. The company leaders expected a consultant to bring solutions so, with the blessings of the sales staff, I took a proposal to the company president and explained why it was a beneficial move.

Because I had specific numbers to show the president how adopting this new policy would positively impact sales, he readily adopted the new quota and proudly conveyed that fact to the sales staff.

By the end of that same year several of the salespeople had actually exceeded the quota by 10% or more—far beyond the current requirement and equal to the previous one. Within a year every member of this seasoned sales staff had exceeded their quotas, which they had been capable of doing all along. The difference was, now the level of annual increase was *their* choice. They had decided what the increase should be and committed to meeting the goal. They were thrilled with being able to take the governors off their selling engines and charge ahead knowing that they wouldn't be penalized for great performance.

If you want to know what will motivate your people, *ask them*. Don't assume you know. If you have created an environment of trust, they will be quite happy to tell you.

CHAPTER FOURTEEN
Exposing the Wizard

When Dorothy and her companions returned to Oz to claim their rewards, they came back with more than just the witch's broom, they had also gathered confidence and determination. They were no longer afraid of the wicked witch (she was dead) or of the wizard. They had proven their worth and now they expected their reward.

This time, the wizard's response, designed to intimidate them into backing down again, didn't work. The transformed team that returned triumphantly with the broom was not the same scared, insecure, ragtag little group that left in search of it. They were bolder, more sure of themselves, and more determined to collect their just rewards, and they were not about to back down. This time they stood their ground and the wizard ended up getting exposed.

Dorothy's transformed team is representative of today's generations. There are many factors driving the behaviors of the new generations, from greater awareness due to global communication and greater access to information, to a bravado born of uncertain times that makes them willing to walk away in order to have what they want.

The new workforce is tapped into the entire world. They know what's going on and they are well aware that employers need employees as much as employees need an employer. This makes the workplace a true arena for negotiation and that fact is not lost on the emerging workforce.

One of the reasons that the newer generations are bolder and less intimidated by the Wizard is because, like little Toto, they are not shy about trekking into once sacred territory and pulling back the curtain to expose what once remained hidden. They are so willing to expose improprieties that not even the clergy or the President of the United States or an oppressive country's dictator is off limits anymore.

Filtering Out Rhetoric

The wealth of information that Gen X and Millennials use to their advantage has, in a curious way, become the undoing of OZ organizations around the world. Information overload has caused these generations, and indeed most all people today, to become very selective about what they allow into their awareness and greater transparency has empowered them to make better decisions.

One of the things the newer generations regularly filter out is rhetoric and what they consider corporate propaganda. Remember, they have already seen what's behind the curtain. They aren't buying into the smoke and mirrors. They see the Wizard for what he is, and they are not impressed.

The newer, more empowered generations are savvier and better informed than any previous generation. Like the transformed Dorothy, they have the courage to call a spade a spade and to challenge the Wizard's behaviors and decisions. They are not content to just pretend things will be alright or to accept the status quo. They are more prone to question authority and expose deceit or fraud than any other generations before them. At their hands entire governments are being toppled.

These tendencies are causing OZ organizations all kinds of grief and they haven't seen anything yet. As Generation X and Millennials dominate the workforce over the next ten to twelve years, organizations that fail to learn how to work with them effectively will find themselves in deep trouble.

There have always been a few brave souls willing to buck a system that is out of touch and unresponsive, but until recently their numbers were very small. The United States would not be an independent country had there not been a few bold and enlightened people willing to risk their lives for truth and justice. Unions would not exist either.

Unfortunately, like the United States government which started out "of the people, by the people, and for the people" and misplaced that idea along the way, many unions have forgotten their original purpose, turned into bureaucracies and have themselves become OZ organizations. So even organizations that purport to be working for the people are suspect to Generation X and Millennials.

It will be interesting to see what occurs in organizations, including unions and the government, as more and more people claim their personal power and refuse to accept the status quo, and as more and more become willing to pull back the curtains and expose deceit.

Of the People, By the People, For the People

With the more enlightened generations, the movement back to the people is gaining momentum. This movement is now multi-generational and no longer confined to "a few good men." Young and old, male and female of every race have begun to storm the castle demanding individual rights and fair consideration, and not just for themselves, but for everyone.

Karen Silkwood, a Boomer, and Erin Brockovich, a Gen Xer, were such people. There is much speculation that Karen Silkwood lost her life as a result of blowing the whistle on the Kerr-McGee plutonium fuels production plant in Crescent, Oklahoma where she worked as a chemical technician.

She suspected that Kerr-McGee was being negligent in maintaining plant safety after she was exposed to plutonium on more than one occasion. Silkwood was a member of the Oil, Chemical, and Atomic Workers' Union and the week prior to her death had reportedly been gathering evidence for the union to support her claim. She was killed in a fatal one-car crash on November 13, 1974 and the circumstances surrounding her death have been the subject of great speculation ever since.

Erin Brockovich took on utility giant Pacific Gas and Electric after discovering that they had been allowing a toxic chemical, Chromium 6, to leak into the groundwater severely compromising the health of countless people who lived in and around Hinkley, California at the time (1960's to 1980's). In 1996, Brockovich and a partner of the small law firm in which she worked as a file clerk brought a class action lawsuit against the giant utility company and won the largest toxic tort injury settlement in U.S. history. Due to her courage and persistence $333 million in damages was paid to more than 600 Hinkley residents.

A more recent example is Dr. David Graham M.D., another Gen Xer and an American epidemiologist. He was a twenty year veteran of the Food and Drug Administration and head of the FDA's Office of Drug Safety when he blew the whistle on Merck's popular anti-inflammatory drug, Vioxx, and uncovered the tragic public health consequences stemming from a legalized conflict of interest between pharmaceuticals and the FDA.

In August 2004, Graham gave his supervisors the results of his research which showed that high-dose prescriptions of the painkiller Vioxx appeared to triple heart attack rates. He suggested that Vioxx needed to be banned. His supervisors responded to the disclosure by telling him to keep quiet. Their reasoning was circular. They held that his findings did not agree with the FDA's position. They told him that, as an employee of the

FDA, his position had to agree with theirs. He couldn't maintain a separate and contradictory position.

Dr. John Jenkins, the FDA director of new drugs, argued that because Graham's findings didn't replicate the drug's warning label, Graham had no grounds for raising the warning. He was told by another supervisor that his position was "particularly problematic since FDA funded this study." Just days after Graham's disclosure, the agency approved Vioxx for use in children.

As it turned out, Graham was right. The following month, Merck pulled Vioxx from the market after its own research found that the drug, even when taken at low dosages, doubled the risk of heart attack. But even with new research and agreement that Vioxx was dangerous, the FDA brass appeared to see Graham as an even greater danger. With a federal hearing on the horizon they knew they couldn't silence the message, so they tried to discredit the messenger. It didn't work.

In November, 2004 Dr. Graham rocked the pharmaceutical industry when the he testified before the U.S. Senate Committee exposing the risks of Vioxx and revealing that a very high number of patients taking high doses of Vioxx suffered heart attacks. "The estimates range from 88,000 to 139,000 Americans," he said. "Of these, 30 to 40 percent probably died. For the survivors, their lives were changed forever" (Berenson 2005).

At the top end of Graham's projections the toll Vioxx took before it was recalled was comparable to the number of Americans killed in Vietnam. In his testimony, Dr. Graham asserted that the policies within the U.S. Food and Drug Administration were not just insufficient to protect the public from drugs which carry unacceptable risks, they actually encouraged their release. He pointed out that, although the FDA was a government run organization created to safeguard the public, the organization's funding depended largely on the success of the pharmaceutical industry—the very industry it is supposed to be regulating. "I would argue that the FDA, as currently configured, is incapable of protecting America against another Vioxx," Graham stated in his testimony. "We are virtually defenseless" (Berenson 2005).

After his testimony, Graham was publicly criticized by the FDA. To protect himself, he contacted the nonprofit whistleblower protection organization, Government Accountability Project (GAP), for advice on getting his findings on Vioxx published over the objections of his superiors. Tom Devine, of GAP, told the Washington Post that "anonymous" callers contacted GAP, apparently working in concert with the FDA, trying to discredit or "smear" Graham, calling him "a demagogue and a bully" and his findings "junk science" (Berenson 2005).

Graham spent his career at the FDA studying the safety of drugs, many of them after FDA approval, using data from medical insurance companies. Besides, Vioxx, Graham was instrumental in removing from the U.S. market the unsafe drugs Omniflox, an antibiotic, Rezulin, a diabetes treatment, Fen-Phen and Redux, weight-loss drugs, and phenylpropanolamine, an over-the-counter decongestant.

Then there are the emboldened young citizens that have taken to the streets in revolt against the oppression in Egypt, Libya and nations all across the planet. Dictatorships are falling fast and they will continue to as the younger generations continue to band together for real change.

Silkwood, Brockovich, Graham, and all the young protesters around the world don't put themselves on the firing line just for themselves. Like Dorothy, they stand their ground on behalf of those who are traveling through life with them and whom they are certain would come to harm without their help.

Until recently, such actions didn't concern the Wizard and his OZites too much because there were so few of these people around, and there were enough Flying Monkeys and Witches to keep them contained. But my, how times have changed! The newer generations don't assume that the Wizard is just one step below God. They don't buy into the top-down hierarchical structure created by OZ organizations, and they are not afraid of the Witch. In greater and greater numbers they are exiting OZ to create their own organizations and they are turning the organizational pyramid upside down.

Turning Organizations Upside-Down

In organizations created by the newer generations employees are seen as being at the top of the pyramid and the leaders at the bottom. Visionary new leaders proudly position themselves as servants to their people. The term "servant leadership" was coined to describe this new leadership style and the idea is rapidly spreading.

The leaders of these bold new companies are collaborative and readily accessible to their people, not as kings and certainly not as invisible wizards, but as equals. Jack Welch was such a leader. When he headed General Electric, and developed his people-centric MBWA management style, it was revolutionary at the time. Under his leadership General Electric went from a market value of $14 billion to one of more than $410 billion, making it the largest and most valuable company in the world at the end of 2004. Welch's style became the standard for many of the more enlightened organizations that began to emerge.

Just a few years back people-centric companies were extremely rare. They are still a very small minority, but they are on the rise and their growth is phenomenal. Many have gone from startup to billion dollar corporations in just a few years because today's best and brightest workers are actively looking for such organizations and will quickly abandon OZ organizations to join them.

Companies like Google, Federal Express, Southwest Airlines, Intuit and Zappos are wildly successful because they are able to attract and keep bright, dedicated, fully engaged people. Contrary to the thinking of many business analysts, well run people-centric companies are not no-consequence cultures where employees are allowed to do anything they please and where they are never fired for misconduct or laid off in down-cycles.

Healthy people-centric companies have taken the time to fully understand human nature and to build a culture that makes the most of it. They are concerned about stockholder returns, just as profit-centric firms are. They are concerned about customers, just as customer-centric firms are. And they are concerned about ideas, just as idea-centric firms are. The difference is that they recognize that great stockholder returns, great customer service and great ideas come from dedicated, enthusiastic, fully engaged employees, so they focus on maintaining a culture that fosters dedication and enthusiasm.

The hard part, and the part that OZ corporations don't bother with, is in taking the time to understand exactly what drives engagement and sustains enthusiasm and dedication both individually and collectively. It takes focused effort on the part of leadership to be sure that each employee is in the right seat, nourished by the right environment, and guided by great leaders.

The leaders of people-centric organizations also know it is well worth the effort because well-placed employees are as much as 800% more effective than those who are misplaced according to a large body of research and in the direct experience of enlightened leaders. It stands to reason that if you are getting 100% from actively engaged employees and 20% or less from actively disengaged ones, productivity and profits are going to increase dramatically when employees are fully engaged.

Old Ways Die Hard

According to a study conducted by Jim Collins, author of *Good to Great,* people-centric organizations generate as much as seven times the revenue of non-people-centric organizations in similar industries. That's *seven hundred percent* more. Surely Wizards see this kind of data, so why aren't they building people-centric companies, and making themselves visible and accessible so they can rake in the profits? Well, it appears that for OZ leaders, it isn't really about profits so much as it is about power and protecting their ego.

Old ways die hard and the Wizard is accustomed to keeping himself hidden away, so although he hears rumors of phenomenal growth and triple digit increases, he doesn't take it too seriously. After all, how can the little people possibly outperform the great OZ? He is certain that they are on a failed mission and that someday they will return to his service and OZ will continue on as before.

What the Wizard fails to consider is that the enlightened new generations already know he's a fraud and they will never be willing to go down that road. With the truth out in the open for everyone to see, OZ organizations have only two choices—fire the Wizard or require that he get out of his fortress and get real.

To survive, today's organizations have to be more organic and less machine-like and hierarchical. OZ has no place in today's world. It is obsolete and outdated. OZ leaders are fooling no one but themselves, and their lack of awareness is proving very costly.

In February 2006, The Dallas Morning News ran an article entitled *Not Quite Golden?* The article examined the high cost of hiring ineffective leaders. Most of the dismissals examined had occurred over less than a two year period. The list included David Edmondson the Radio Shack CEO that got fired after nine months. His severance package cost the company 1.5 million dollars, and the company suffered 2.5 billion in stock losses under Edmondson's leadership. Also listed were Phillip Purcell (Morgan Stanley) whose severance package cost $43.9 million, Carly Fiorina (Hewlett-Packard)—cost $21 million, J. Michael Lawrie (Siebel Systems)—cost 4.5 million and Mary Forte (Zales Corp.)—cost $8.5 million.

Less than a year later The New York Times ran an article covering the firing of JC Penney COO, Catherine West. The cost? Over ten million dollars (Moore 2007).

Were these people inept or were the organizations too out of touch with today's needs to allow them to function? From the outside looking in, there is really no way to know for sure, but there are clues.

On the one hand, we can assume that people hired for such important top positions in big corporations go though all kinds of screening. On the other, we can see that none of the organizations are new, cutting edge, truly people-centric organizations. All are old, established, publicly traded companies that answer first and foremost to their stockholders. That doesn't necessarily mean that the dismissed executives were without blame, but surely they came in the door apparently having the right stuff. We can't know for sure what happened, but we can know that there was a serious disconnect somewhere.

OZ organizations tend to be disconnected and dysfunctional on many levels, and it is not uncommon for the dysfunction to start at the recruiting level. When an organization is focused on dollars and believes that technical skills are the answer to ensuring a healthy bottom line, their focus is primarily on technical skills.

How emotionally healthy the people they place in leadership positions are, or how effectively they connect with and inspire people are rarely considered beyond surface measures. Yet, in leadership, these skills are far more important than technical skills.

With their typical approach to performance problems being to provide training and more training based on what the leaders have determined the errant employee needs, it is no wonder that seemingly good candidates, even top level ones, frequently fall short of expectations.

Because OZ leaders are generally focused on the wrong things, they frequently make the wrong decisions. It is so much easier to fire employees that training fails to "fix" than it is to look at their own toxic environment or at themselves, even if it does cost millions of dollars and destroy lives.

CHAPTER FIFTEEN
Goodbye Yellow Brick Road

Elton John's song, *Goodbye Yellow Brick Road,* begins with the lyrics, "When are you gonna come down? When are you going to land?" The refrain is "Goodbye Yellow Brick Road where the dogs of society howl. You can't plant me in your penthouse. I'm going back to my plow... I've finally decided my future lies beyond the Yellow Brick Road."

This refrain pretty much sums up the attitudes of the younger generations. Unlike earlier generations, more and more of the new workforce are deciding that their future lies beyond the constraints of OZ.

They really would rather "go back to the plow" so to speak, than deal with the restrictions and lack of consideration they find in OZ organizations. They look at the outdated rules that are prevalent in far too many organizations and they are unwilling to follow them. They see how shallow all the pomp and ceremony is and they are not the least bit interested in playing that game.

Though OZ organizations tend to see Generation X and Millennials as undisciplined and lacking in a strong work ethic; as disloyal and fickle, having interviewed literally thousands of them over the past twelve years, what we consistently find is that the vast majority express a strong desire to be of service. They want to do something *significant*; to be high performers who make a real difference, not just in a company, but in the world.

These generations are technically savvy and, having grown up in the world of gaming, have learned very good strategy and decision-making skills, which they want to put to good use.

A New Model of Winning and Losing

Gaming gave the last half of Generation X and all of the Millennial generation a completely different paradigm around winning and losing than previous generations had. Previous generations learned about winning and losing from sports and war models where there were set rules, a clear distinction between winners and losers, and where the players were expected to stick with the game or the battle until the end even if they were losing.

The gaming model uses strategies to work through a maze of new and unexpected situations. If you play the game right, you are always on the winning side and the losers are inconsequential. In gaming, if you get too far off track or find yourself in a situation where it appears you cannot win, you simply reset the game, learn from your mistakes and correct them on the next run through.

If you are good at remembering what you did wrong and avoid doing that again, you keep moving to higher and higher levels until you finally outsmart the game and win. If you are in a hurry to advance, there are "cheats" available that help you discover how to maneuver better and get farther faster. And there is no stigma in using the cheat sheets to get ahead. It's just good gaming.

That's exactly what the new generations are doing in the workplace too. They want to go as far as they can as fast as they can and, if things look like they are not going as planned and there is no way to win, they RESET, learn from their mistakes and start over.

This is actually a really great model when you look at it with unjaundiced eyes. The fast-thinking, strategy-based, problem-solving mindset is exactly what organizations need in the fast-paced, global marketplace we live in today. These are the very things that will give organizations an edge.

Though the younger generations love their kind of gaming, they have a strong aversion to the kind of game playing and rules OZ type organizations employ. Because the newer generations see right through the games and refuse to play, OZ leaders see the new generations as problem employees.

At the moment OZ leaders are soothing themselves with comments like, "These kids have a lot to learn. Hopefully, they will grow up someday and get with the program." What they are really saying is that someday these young people will stop acting like Gen Xers and Millennials and start acting more like Traditionals. WRONG! They will never act or think like Traditionals. Those days are gone. And the sooner OZ leaders figure this out, the better off everyone will be.

Fearless and Flexible

Both Generation X and Millennials are more fearless than previous generations and more prone to stand up for themselves. Generation X has that odd label because of their aversion to labels, to rules or to anything else they think will restrict them or limit their options.

They grew up in a world where corruption and ineptness at both governmental and corporate levels permeated the news and they came to believe at a very early age that they had no safety net. They are certain, for instance, that the Social Security system is in trouble and will not be there for them when they retire. They don't believe that top leaders can be trusted to help and they see a government in shambles.

They barely trusted those at the helm before the events of September 11, 2001. That event was pivotal in convincing them that they were on their own; that they could not even depend on the government to keep them safe, much less to help them succeed.

They do not believe that life for them will be better than life for their parents, and they have decided that their only option for happiness is to claim it now whenever and wherever they can. Generation X lives for today and makes no apologies for that fact. When you grow up believing there are no guarantees of anything, that you have to depend on your own resources, and that you only get what you go after, succumbing to fear is not an option.

Millennials have grown up in an era of terrorism, both at home and world-wide. Like Generation X, their world has always been one of uncertainty. But, where Generation X decided to deal with the uncertainty by living full out right now, Millennials are looking further into the future and asking very deep questions. They consider the effects of true heroism, patriotism, and civic engagement, and want to be a part of that grander vision. For them, the uncertainty and the threat of terrorism is a reminder of the importance of community and connectivity, and of the need to act heroically.

Millennials have decided to step up to the plate in a way few generations before them have done. They are more socially and civic-minded than previous generations and more likely to volunteer their time and energy to a cause they believe in. They want to do more than just participate, they want to contribute in some meaningful way. Millennials exhibit a strong social conscience and they expect the companies they work for to be both socially and environmentally responsible. To work for an organization that fails to meet their high standards goes against their values and they have no problem hitting the reset button, leaving the offender behind and starting over.

Money is not the motivator for this generation that it has been for previous generations. They want meaning and purpose and, unless organizations learn to provide that in authentic ways, today's workers—especially the most talented ones—will be saying "goodbye" in greater and greater numbers.

Somewhere, over the rainbow, skies are blue
and the dreams that you dare to dream really do come true...

Someday I'll wish upon a star
and wake up where the clouds are far behind me...

Lyrics from *Over the Rainbow*

CHAPTER SIXTEEN
Realities and Rewards

Workplace studies suggest that the average manager spends almost eighty percent of their time trying to keep employees directed and productive. They complain that this leaves them too little time for other important tasks. This produces a lot of frustration and stress, and when stress mounts the majority of managers do not handle it well.

Some step away from their people in order to handle other duties and a no-consequences culture develops. Some get stricter and stricter with employees, trying to rein them in and minimize bad behaviors and a no-mistakes culture develops. Some try to do it all themselves and a firefighter culture develops. In all three instances the stress levels of both managers and employees continue to rise. As stress levels rise, productivity falls and the vicious cycle gains greater momentum.

At some point something has got to give and what gives is very detrimental to the organization. Employees start taking more and more sick days. They are disengaged when at work and working at 40% of their capacity, or less. Eventually the best employees start leaving in search of a less stressful workplace. Managers are then left with the least resourceful employees, which further exacerbates the problem. If managers don't get the training they need to be able to effectively deal with the new reality of employee management, the better of them leave in search of a less stressful environment as well.

The cost of replacing a lost line worker is estimated at 1.5 times the employee's salary. The cost of replacing a manager is estimated at between 5 and 7 times their salary. Lose too many employees and any potential profits walk right out the door with them. Keep disengaged employees and the cost due to lost productivity can be even more costly. Most workers leave an organization because they have become disengaged for one reason or another. The answer then is not to keep recruiting, hiring, and firing, but to keep engaging.

Although most companies are at a loss as to why the costly turnover trend continues, evidence suggests that, in many cases, the companies themselves, in an effort to stem employee dissatisfaction and avoid lawsuits, are inadvertently creating the very problems they are trying to stem.

There are four primary factors that determine employee outcomes. These are:

1. Leadership

2 Environment or company culture

3. Employees' attributes

4. Employees' attitudes

Each interacts with the others and affects them to a large degree. Ultimately, all four factors must be aligned for optimal performance. How adequately these categories are addressed and managed determines, almost entirely, how effectively an organization and its employees will function. In too many organizations, however, three of the four factors (2 through 4) are rarely given sufficient attention which adversely affects leadership, causing malfunctions around all four factors.

To better understand how these four factors affect OZ organizations, and how they may be affecting yours, we will briefly examine each of them.

Leadership

Most organizations understand the value of good leadership and are willing to invest in the development of their management staff. The problem is that they are often throwing money away on programs that fail to teach managers how to manage in today's world. Rather than addressing the realities, many management programs rely on the old tried and true techniques; techniques that worked in the slower-paced, more predictable industrial age, but that do not work today, as many "well trained" managers who struggle to manage their staff are discovering.

While larger, more established corporations with deeper pockets can generally survive a few incompetent leaders, the dreadful financial numbers of many of today's corporate giants and the demise of several multi-national organizations point to the fact that ineffective leadership in any organization can be devastating.

Poor managers can quickly destroy the morale of an entire department, and at the executive level, of the entire organization. Where morale is lacking, so too is respect, dedication, ingenuity, forethought, productivity and just about everything else necessary to organizational success. Under self-absorbed, detached leaders, employees are usually just putting in their time and watching their backs.

Great leaders are great because they are competent—not necessarily at managing systems, they have dependable employees who can do that—but at understanding and developing their people.

The primary indicators of a great leader are strong people skills and a high degree of emotional intelligence or self-management. Great leaders know that to get exemplary performance from their employees, they must first model it.

The higher the leadership position, the more critical good interpersonal skills become. Yet, OZ organizations tend to devalue "soft" skills training. They prefer to invest in "hard" skills, those they think directly impact operations. But, at a leadership level "soft" skills impact operations far more than technical or "hard" skills. Without good people skills, leaders and managers will always face huge challenges that they cannot solve.

Hard Skills

Hard skills encompass technical or administrative procedures related to an organization's core business. Examples include computer protocols, administrative and financial procedures, sales techniques, administration, machine operation, and safety standards. Hard skills are typically easy to observe, qualify, quantify, and measure. And they are easier to train than soft skills, because in most instances the skills being taught are brand new to the learner so they don't have to unlearn something before they can start learning.

Soft Skills

By contrast, soft skills, while easy to observe, are not so easy to qualify, quantify and measure. Moreover, no one gets to the workplace with a clean slate, so unlearning almost always has to occur before new learning can take effect. With soft skills, training may take longer, and with return on investment being harder to measure, many OZ leaders see soft skills as too "squishy". Yet it is the presence or absence of healthy interpersonal skills, especially in leadership, that typically make or break an organization.

Soft skills are all about people, and so too is effective leadership. Soft skills include effective self-management (management of emotions, coping skills, stress management, etc.), the ability to relate to others effectively, good communication skills, including listening, the ability to engage in meaningful dialogue and give good feedback.

The ability to contribute and cooperate as a team member, to problem solve, make good decisions, resolve conflict, negotiate and persuade, and to cope with stressors effectively all develop through soft skills training.

Leaders at all levels rely on these skills far more than they rely on hard skills. Through the effective use of soft skills, leaders set good examples of behavioral protocol, build teams, facilitate meetings, solve problems, make decisions, plan, delegate, encourage, persuade, inspire, motivate, instruct, coach, and guide innovation.

Clearly no leader can be effective without these skills. Leaders who are spending their time and energy on the hard skills are not really leaders; they are technicians masquerading as leaders. We could perhaps consider them managers, but they are managing processes more than people. Firefighter managers are usually relying on their hard skills more than soft skills and, in doing so, are creating the very fire-storms they are trying so hard to contain.

Most soft skills are learned through observation and experimentation, not in a classroom. Lacking any formal training in this area, people tend to try many things and then stick with what seems to work best for them. Much of what we learn in life's arena is effective and useful, but much of what we adopt informally can create more problems that it solves.

It has been our experience, and from the feedback we get, the experience of most managers that, without training to develop and enhance soft skills, the majority of people are not very effective in areas that require them. What is learned on the streets rarely results in fully functioning, high performance employees.

Environment and Company Culture

Every company has its own particular culture. Company cultures are perceived as slow-paced or fast-paced, highly structured or flexible, strict or relaxed, employee-centered or process-centered.

Even in the healthiest of cultures, there will be certain types of employees who fit within it better than others. It is extremely useful to know both the company culture and which employees best fit it, and how to effectively manage those who don't naturally fit.

When an organization's culture falls somewhere between healthy and mediocre, employee morale and problems are fairly manageable. In the three types of culture that are decidedly unhealthy, that is not the case.

In the no-mistakes culture, in which everyone is called out on the carpet for any little mistake, employees are overly cautious, vigilant, stressed out and emotionally disengaged. In this instance disengagement occurs through fear.

In the no-consequence culture, which on the surface might seem to be a laid-back, easy-going environment, employees are not managed effectively, slackers and trouble-makers are tolerated, and potentially good employees are stressed and frustrated. Employees disengage in a no-consequence culture because they have little incentive to perform beyond minimal levels.

In the firefighter culture everyone is too busy juggling projects and dealing with emergencies to communicate, cooperate, develop a good work plan or improve their outcomes. In this culture employees disengage because they are frustrated, confused, stressed out and always on the edge of burnout.

Turnover tends to be very high in all three cultures. In the no-mistakes and firefighter cultures, both productive and non-productive employees leave. In the no-consequence culture slackers tend to stay because they are alright with not being productive. Those who want to be productive are the ones that leave.

In a healthy culture everyone from the CEO to the janitor communicate, cooperate, and participate in achieving the company's goals. One of the company's goals is to have happy, engaged employees. In healthy cultures employees feel heard, appreciated and informed. Organizational transparency and employee feedback are standards so not only do employees know what is going on in the organization at any given time, they help shape it. Leaders both model high performance and expect it from their people. Their leadership style is that of a good coach and the coaching model is the standard for leaders on every level. Employees are held to a high standard which is clearly conveyed and consistently adhered to and, because the standard ensures fairness and respect, employees are fully engaged and committed to performing to the standard conveyed.

Employee Attributes

While no two people are exactly alike, all people fall into particular classifications that are useful in defining them and their abilities. The classifications generally used in the workplace, such as gender, age, education level, and work experience, are ultimately far less important than the less regularly used classifications of personality type, natural traits and abilities, behavioral styles, coping capacity, values, emotional maturity and character.

Many OZ organizations never bother with the latter classifications at all. OZ leaders see these attributes as incidental to getting the job done. Nothing could be further from the truth. Volumes of research data, such as the broad study done by U.C. San Diego professor, Dr. Judith Bardwick, clearly proves that character and personality influence behaviors and outcomes on the job more than knowledge and skills. Dr. Bardwick states that it is much easier for an individual to learn new skills and information than it is to change an individual's personality and character; to make a timid person bold, for example (Bardwick 1998).

The fact is, it is impossible to change the natural, primary traits of people. We can enforce certain behaviors, but we cannot make those who struggle to maintain those behaviors enjoy them, be motivated by them, or be effective in performing them.

Everyone has natural resistance to their least preferred traits and, in trying to sustain them, they burn up huge amounts of energy that leave them drained and disinterested. This excess expenditure of energy can be seen in workplace lethargy and has even been documented in lab experiments.

Using PET scan studies, Dr. Richard Haier of UC Irvine School of Medicine demonstrated that the brain works much harder when an individual is not using naturally preferred functions. In PET scans areas of the brain "burn hot" when people are developing new skills or using skills outside their area of natural proficiency. Dr. Haier estimates that the brain works as much as 100 times harder in these situations and uses up vast stores of energy (Haier and Jung 2007).

Such studies point to the extreme importance of getting the right people in the right seats, not just in leadership positions, but in all positions. There are few things an organization can do that will improve performance outcomes more than getting the right people in the right positions. This is especially critical when selecting people for leadership roles. Unfortunately, few organizations are doing this. Not because they don't want to, but because the methods they insist on using rarely yield the necessary data to make a truly informed decision. So getting the right people in the right seats has proven to be a far bigger order than most employers have been able to manage.

Emotional Intelligence - A Necessary Attribute

Character and competence, two primary components to employee success, do not occur where emotional maturity is lacking. Author and researcher Daniel Goleman brought the critical importance of the factor called "emotional intelligence" to popularity in his book by the same name. *Emotional Intelligence* cites study after study that shows emotional intelligence (EQ) to be a greater predictor of outstanding performance in the workplace than education and technical training combined, and the top predictor of overall goal achievement.

What is rarely addressed in typical EQ assessments and training, is naturally preferred attributes and whether there is what Swiss psychologist, Carl Jung, called falsification of type. It is an important aspect of the equation because people rarely develop a healthy degree of emotional intelligence when they are working against their naturally preferred traits.

Failure to get to the core of employee motivation, which derives from natural traits, and to ensure that employees are working with, rather than against their natural abilities is what causes much of the high stress and low productivity found in so many organizations.

As a psychologist, coach, consultant, trainer, and the originator of the deep analysis system, the *CORE Multidimensional Awareness Profile*® (CORE MAP), I have seen tens of thousands of instances of well-educated, experienced employees who are highly problematical and unproductive due to poor development of naturally preferred traits and emotional immaturity. Almost all organizational and interpersonal problems revolve around these two factors.

In one international organization I worked with, a group of managers had done a study that measured levels of employee training against overall effectiveness. The company had placed employees into four quadrants: high training-high effectiveness (HH), high training-low effectiveness (HL), low training-high effectiveness (LH), and low training-low effectiveness (LL). To their dismay nearly two-thirds of their workforce fell into the high training, low effectiveness group. They were baffled as to why all the training they had provided was not producing more effective employees.

In looking at their culture and management philosophies, and at the fact that they had done little to ensure that they had the right people in the right seats, the reasons for the high degree of employee ineffectiveness became quite clear.

First, they were trying to train people to fit the jobs because they had no reliable means for determining which people naturally fit them. They were essentially trying to teach eagles to burrow and moles to fly. Moreover, their culture was unstable. There were areas where no mistakes were tolerated and areas where there were no consequences for poor performance. Employees were treated differently from one another and from situation to situation. There was little consistency and no predictability. Because there were no clear guidelines for managers or employees to follow, managers were frequently operating, more or less, by the seat of their pants and employees were trying to figure things out as they went.

Many employees had no idea how the work they did every day impacted the company as a whole. They just did the job and collected a paycheck. For these employees, there was no pride in their work because they could not see its value, and there was no motivation to do better.

While managers tried to acknowledge their employees, the employees rarely felt that they were acknowledged in any genuine way. The common consensus was that the company didn't really see their contributions, which was true because their contributions were usually based on what employees assumed leaders wanted, but were as often as not quite different than what company leaders, who had failed to communicate, intended.

Like many such organizations, the company believed that the answer to poor performance was additional training. They had a mechanisitic view of their workforce which held that an under-performing "machine" would operate better if the mechanical parts (the systems) were well oiled and the machine tuned up. In other words, if systems were improved and the employees trained to manage the systems better.

Organizations are really living systems, not machines and the employees understood this. So where the employees were trying to breathe life into a project, the managers were trying to oil the machine. They were on completely different missions and no one had bothered to look deeply enough to even know this was happening, much less find out why.

Unstable cultures, which usually incorporate one or more of the unhealthy cultural styles, almost never produce top performers. And the top performers that land in these cultures don't stay long. And since the newer generations are much quicker to abandon unhealthy cultures than previous generations, the problem is growing more prevalent.

Employee Attitudes

Bad attitudes in employees can almost always be traced to poor leadership practices and/or an unhealthy environment. Remember the attitudes of the employees in the chapter one story where top management was disconnected, unresponsive, and too immature and self-absorbed to hear what the employees were trying to convey? When leaders substitute real connectedness and communication with "Rah! Rah! Let's get fired up!" platitudes, bad attitudes are inevitable. The first place to look then, is at leadership practices.

Leaders are not always to blame, of course. Many people bring their problems from home to work and proceed to share them with anyone who will allow it. Other people are just plain difficult all the time. But these behaviors can only continue if leaders put up with them, so we still have to come back to leadership where problem attitudes persist.

Leaders can create bad attitudes or they can allow them to persist, and in either case, the buck needs to stop there. This is typically a leadership problem however, not a management problem. Managers often want to solve attitude problems and would if they could, but organizational rules imposed by disconnected OZ bureaucracies prevent it.

When OZ leaders are too focused on processes, procedures and profits to give sufficient consideration to their people, they can create a lot of internal problems; from disengaged, unproductive employees to those that are actively sabotaging the organization.

When employees feel overlooked and unappreciated, generally some of them will complain to their managers, but in OZ organizations, managers feel powerless to change the prevailing culture so they respond to employee complaints with what appears to be indifference, which causes the employees to develop indifference toward the manager and the company.

Employee indifference leads to disengagement and lower levels of performance. The lowered performance leads to lower profits, which leads to directives from the Wizard to tighten controls. Managers try to comply, which further alienates the employees and tensions escalate. This vicious cycle continues to increase and feed upon itself until a tornado-like environment develops and everyone goes into hyper-vigilance. From there, everyone is more concerned with survival than performance and things spiral down even further.

As long as the OZ leader stays disconnected and unapproachable, the problem grows and attitudes continue to deteriorate. Anytime you see a general malaise and wide-spread poor attitudes among employees, you can bet this sort of thing is happening.

When just one department is dysfunctional, it might be because the manager of that department is dysfunctional or it might be that there is a problem employee with a bad attitude keeping everyone else stirred up and off-balance. Like one bad apple, one bad attitude can spoil the whole bunch given enough time and latitude—and one is generally all it takes. This can only continue as long as it is tolerated by leadership however.

Because the causes of employee problems can be broad and varied, and each of the four factors impacts the others, the exact cause may at first be hard to pinpoint. But, whatever the cause, the good news is, it's curable. But it must always be cured at its source, and the source is always top level leadership. New systems, re-engineering, quality circles, team-building exercises, incentives, raises, and all the other things that are commonly tried will be temporary fixes at best unless the source of the problem is addressed and healed.

Healing comes from deep understanding. Understanding brings cooperation and cooperation fosters good working relationships. Good working relationships produce results, better results improve productivity, and greater productivity increases profits. The path to real and lasting productivity and profits is that of cultivating exceptional employees. It is the one path that is too often overlooked and yet the only one that leads surely and predictably to many great returns.

CHAPTER SEVENTEEN
Oz Never Did Give Nothing to the Tin Man

> Back where I come from, there are men who do nothing all day but good deeds... And their hearts are no bigger than yours – *But!* They have one thing you haven't got. A testimonial. Therefore, in consideration of your kindness, I take pleasure at this time in presenting you with a small token of our esteem and affection. And remember, my sentimental friend, that a heart is not judged by how much you love, but by how much you are loved by others.
>
> The Wizard of Oz to the Tin Man

In the song *Tin Man*, by America, the observation that "Oz never did give nothing to the Tin Man that he didn't . . . already have" presents an important truth. The only thing Oz ever gave, and all any leader *can* give, is greater awareness of innate traits and abilities, the kind of encouragement that leads to confidence, and the right conditions for optimal performance and growth.

The Scarecrow had a brain all along, the Tin Man had a heart, the Lion had courage and Dorothy had a way home. The same is true of all those people in OZ organizations who appear to be lacking the means to succeed.

The reality is that we all come into the world as bundles of potential. Potential that, if fully realized, provides each of us with everything we need to be absolutely amazing. People aren't brainless, heartless or lacking in courage because they choose to be. They are there because they lack awareness and/or training in some essential area.

When training compliments natural traits and abilities, improvement is rapid and profound. But, when we are doing the equivalent of trying to teach moles to fly and eagles to burrow, the mole and eagle both look inept and the trainer incompetent.

No one is fatally flawed by nature. Those that appear to be are functioning far below their potential, and are typically not managing stress very well, but both problems can be quickly eliminated under the right conditions.

Just as Dorothy and her companions went seeking what they thought they needed to be fully functional, so too does the average person. People almost universally want to function at their best and, when they don't, there are very specific reasons why. In the workplace there are three primary reasons:

1. **Low self-awareness** – When employees don't know themselves well enough to report their true nature or to choose a career that compliments it, they often go into whatever line of work seems easiest or most lucrative, or they accept whatever position is available in an organization.

Some luck into the right work, but most don't. Approximately 58% of US workers report that they are dissatisfied with their job. And, not surprisingly, the lowest levels of job satisfaction are among younger workers. A survey of more than 5,000 U. S. workers, conducted in 2007 by the Conference Board, a New York-based private research group found that only 39 percent of respondents aged 25 and younger said they liked their current jobs. According to the report, this is the lowest level in the survey's 20-year history. Job satisfaction for workers between the ages of 45 and 54 was at 45 percent. The best scores, and the ones that made the overall score look deceptively better, came from older workers, aged 55 and older (MSNBC.com 2007).

2. **Low self-management and self-worth** – Low self-management includes low levels of emotional intelligence, low tolerance for non-preferred tasks, poor interpersonal skills, poor coping mechanisms, and immature attitudes and behaviors. Low self-worth includes lack of self-confidence, low self-esteem and limiting beliefs about one's abilities. Any of these factors can greatly diminish effectiveness and increase the need for close management. People who cannot manage their emotions and interactions are almost always difficult employees. Some are too passive, some passive-aggressive and some aggressive, but all add to management woes in some way.

People who lack confidence in their ability to perform generally will not risk stepping out and trying anything new or extending themselves into more challenging work. They perform below their capacity and are typically not motivated to do better. Without training and/or coaching to correct the low self-appraisals, these employees will continue to need external motivation.

3. **The workplace itself** – Workplace factors (poor leadership, unhealthy work environment and/or being placed into the wrong job) have already been examined. This is the first place any organization should look, but certainly not the only place. Even in supportive work environments employees who lack self-awareness, self-confidence or effective self-management will never become the star performers organizations seek.

Before employees can perform to capacity, they and their leaders must know what "capacity" really is. It is not merely education and experience. These are simply a collection of learned skills. Learned skills certainly add to the capacity to perform, provided they do not conflict with natural inclinations. When they do, the natural inclinations will almost always win out.

Learned skills (education and experience) are critical to good outcomes, but they are just one part of the equation. There are many other factors that need to be addressed.

When employers realize that they cannot give employees attributes that they don't already have, perhaps they will pay more attention to discovering and developing natural attributes, and less to trying to shape people to the available jobs.

Many organizations undervalue training because their experience has been that training too often results in unsatisfactory outcomes. This is not surprising in light of the fact that managers typically determine who gets training and on what they will be trained without ever consulting the employees to find out what they think they need to learn to be most effective.

Before people are willing to learn they must be interested in the subject matter. The way training is typically done, the odds are very high that the majority of people in the classroom have no interest in being there. How is training typically done? A manager decides that his or her team needs training for some reason; maybe they are not working together as a team in the way the manager thinks they should be; maybe they are not as enthusiastic about the new project as the manager thinks they should be; maybe it has been awhile since employees have had any training and the company encourages "continual improvement". For whatever reason, the manager decides training would be beneficial and contacts the OD department or one of the company's training vendors. They decide what the training should be and arrange to have the entire team attend.

Usually, the employees have little-to-no say in this process. In fact, in many organizations regular training is required and the organization decides what it should be. Worse yet, the training is frequently delivered via online programs where the employees are required to sit in front of a computer and learn something they may or may not be interested in, and in which they may or may not need improvement.

Statistics for the effectiveness of computer-based training consistently show that this form of training is less effective than classroom training, as the Croft-Baker and Zielinski studies cited in chapter nine show. This is no surprise either. At least in a classroom setting, the participant has the advantage of being in a different environment and of the energy and feedback from a group. Both of these factors increase the odds that the participant will be exposed to something of interest.

Research suggests that in the United States 73% of the population is naturally extroverted, and extroverts learn best through discussion and hands on experience. They also enjoy a change of scene, interactive learning and a lot of variety.

For the action-oriented extrovert, online training is fine as long as there is plenty of opportunity for hands-on learning and meeting new challenges experientially. For the socially-oriented extrovert, computer-based training is generally too solitary. If it has lots of stories, analogies, color, pizzazz and experiential exercises, it is more appealing, but the sociable extroverts need interaction so, unless the training is conducted in a classroom with a group of people and combined with discussion, it is usually not very appealing.

The primary problem though is that organizations don't tend to begin training where they should, with understanding the needs and requirements of each employee. Except for well designed team building training that considers and addresses the interests, strengths and limitations of every team member, most general training is lost on the majority of participants because it does not interest them for one reason or another.

To get the best from each and every employee it is essential to know what each one brings to the table; that is, what they have already developed to healthy levels, what they would benefit from developing and what they are interested in developing. In other words, enhancing the strengths and abilities they already have rather than trying to add something they don't need and will not use.

CHAPTER EIGHTEEN
There's No Place Like Home

In the ideal home, a two year old is not expected to have the same skills, abilities and understanding as a teenager, and the teenager is not expected to have the same skills, abilities and understanding as the adults.

The teenager is held to a higher standard than the two year old and, as long as that standard is fair, it actually acts as a motivator because, when the higher standard is met, it is rewarded with greater freedom and autonomy. Both the teenager and the two year old are expected to learn and show continual improvement consistent with their potential, but neither is ever confused with the other.

In a healthy family environment, the parents are dedicated to ensuring the success of the children as they grow into adulthood. They help when and where they need to, but mostly provide the structure, support and teaching that allow the children to grow into well adjusted, independent, fully functioning adults.

In organizations, this same dynamic is essential for optimal functioning. This is the environment in which almost all humans function best, even as adults.

People need to be valued as individuals and trusted to perform to their capacity. They need enough freedom and flexibility to grow, and enough structure and informed guidance to make good decisions and actively contribute to the group in meaningful ways.

Employees also need clear boundaries. They need to know exactly what benefits they will receive from adhering to the prescribed rules, and they need to know the personal and collective consequences for not adhering to them.

For optimal buy-in and motivation, both the rewards and the consequences must be clearly spelled out, perceived as fair, fully adhered to, and meted out consistently.

A Healthy Balance

Healthy organizations maintain a good balance between flexibility and boundaries. They have a clear vision of who they are and what they are about and they convey this to employees consistently. They know where they are headed and why. They are on a mission that has meaning. They are very transparent in that they openly convey their vision, their mission, their goals, and their means of measuring progress. They are also clear and unambiguous about their position. All relevant information is conveyed openly and freely to all employees.

Employees are engaged because they are included in the vision. They know the part they play in the realization of the mission, and they know the importance of carrying out their part. They know the reason for every initiative and the steps they must take to ensure that goals are met. They are privy to the organization's performance measures, including financial measures, so they know how their actions impact them, their team, and the entire organization for good or ill.

Employees in healthy organizations are also given choices. They have a say in how projects proceed and feel that their ideas and opinions count. They are not afraid to speak their mind, or even to disagree when they believe it is in their best interest, or the best interest of their team or the organization. And, when they disagree, they feel like they are actually heard and their position considered.

Almost universally people describe the right fit as a company that values employees, not just for what they can do for the company's bottom line, but as human beings with wants, needs, feelings and valid opinions. They want a company with a heart as well as a brain. They want leaders they can trust. They want to work for a company that values their contribution and fairly compensates them for it. They want the company they call home and the people who lead it to have the courage to step out into the open and tell the truth.

They want to hear the bad news as well as the good and to have the opportunity to decide whether they believe in the vision, mission, and goals enough to fight the good fight or make the necessary sacrifices to ensure the company's survival. They want the opportunity to help meet the challenges their employer faces. They want their leaders to listen, to admit when they don't know, to be vulnerable and real, as well as courageous. They want their leaders to have the wisdom to think things through before they commit and the integrity to stay with their commitments once they make them. They want to know that their leaders will never promise anything that they are not sure they can deliver on. They want leaders they can be proud to follow.

A Culture that Works

Years ago many organizations tried to adopt the Japanese management style. In most cases it failed miserably and far too many companies went back to the old command and control style, which doesn't work anymore either.

The reason the Japanese management style doesn't work in American corporations is because Americans have different ethics than the Japanese. The work ethic, community ethic, family ethic, and value systems are all quite different.

In Japan, community and honor are highly respected and revered. Part of honor is doing the "right thing", even when no one is watching—and the "right thing" is clearly defined. In such a culture it is safe and even wise to allow the people to work together in a community-like structure where they govern themselves with minimal supervision. Their upbringing has prepared them to honor and respect such an arrangement.

In America independence, freedom, and autonomy are highly prized. It's a "do your own thing" culture, yet one that imposes rules and guidelines dictated by a puritanical parental model, cookie-cutter schools, fundamental religions, and the laws of the land. This odd combination engenders a population where the majority wants to work independently yet collaborate as necessary; wants clear guidelines for what is expected of them yet the autonomy, freedom and flexibility to get results independently.

To many Americans, Japanese management is too dependent on cooperation and discussion, and not dependent enough on good leadership. Americans want clear guidelines and directives from collaborative leaders, and then the freedom to work within those guidelines in their own way.

For that formula to work effectively, it is crucial that employees are properly placed according to their natural abilities and given responsibilities in direct proportion to their emotional maturity and overall development.

Few organizations address these two essential elements, and many don't even know that they should. Even organizations who regularly use assessments, are often not measuring for these two critical factors. One reason is because most assessments don't reveal these factors, and batteries of tests that are more comprehensive are too expensive and time consuming.

The limitations of most of the assessments on the market are why the CORE system of assessment and analysis was developed. The *CORE Multidimensioal Awareness Profile* (CORE MAP) does the work of a battery of tests at a fraction of the time and expense and measures for both overall development and emotional intelligence as well as natural abilities, strengths, and competencies, and predicts motivation and stress responses under a wide variety of circumstances.

Since undeveloped, emotionally immature employees can wreak havoc at any level and can destroy entire organizations at senior levels, addressing these factors is critical. Emotionally immature employees are the primary source of petty politics, time-wasting, gossip, loafing, slacking off, failed projects, departmental silos, conflict and a host of other counter-productive behaviors.

CORE Analysis

Emotional Intelligence (EQ) is touted as the number one predictor of effectiveness, yet research using the CORE MAP analysis system consistently shows that effective traits development is directly correlated with EQ. So, although EQ is an essential factor, it is not more important than the effective development of positive traits. In fact, it appears you cannot have one without the other.

It might stand to reason that improving one will improve the other, and that is true. But trying to improve EQ without correcting the factors that are leading to immature or negative behaviors it is pretty much like trying to cure pneumonia by treating the cough. The underlying condition will continue to create problems until it is addressed and eliminated.

When discovering natural traits and placing employees accordingly is not part of the hiring and placement process, employees regularly get put into the wrong jobs. According to our research, this frequently occurs because most assessments have no means for separating conditioned behaviors from natural ones, and the conditioned ones are the ones most frequently reported.

Decades of research on thousands of subjects suggests that nearly 84% of the population misreport on most assessments. The tendency of this very large percentage to report conditioned, observable behaviors rather than natural ones occurs because the natural ones have been masked by conditioning, usually since early childhood, and are not readily observable—neither by self nor others.

Many people know how to skew most assessments, but most skewing does not occur intentionally. The majority of people are trying to be perfectly honest. They just don't know what their truth is so can't report it.

To understand how this occurs, consider "handedness". Suppose you were born left-handed in a world, such as the Middle-East, where predominant use of the left hand was forbidden.

In this world, every time you reached for something with your left hand, that hand would get slapped or pulled back. Before you were a year old, you would have figured out that using your left hand was not acceptable and you would cease to use it as your dominant hand.

If you were then asked as an adult whether you were born right or left handed, you would honestly answer "right-handed". You would have no knowledge of having been born left-handed because that was conditioned out of you too early for you to remember.

Now suppose you used your dominant left hand until you were nine or ten years old and then sustained an injury that prevented its use which forced you to use your right hand instead. In this case, if an assessment asked whether you were born right or left-handed, you would report "left-handed" and could explain why you now use your right hand instead. But, if the assessment merely asked (as many do) whether you were currently using your right or left hand, you would still report right-handedness because in that moment, that is the truth.

It wasn't always the truth, and is not the hand that, given the right training, would be the most functional, but if the assessment was not looking deeply enough to find a natural ability rather than a current behavior, that natural ability would not be reported.

The same happens all the time when using typical assessments to determine job fit. Knowing the natural traits of employees is extremely important because conditioning does not drive performance. Nature does. Conditioning that complements nature can certainly *improve* performance, but it does not *drive* it.

Failure to perform can often be traced right back to employees doing work for which they have learned skills, but possess no natural inclinations. Even the other two great performance drainers (poor leadership and culture) can be traced right back to this if we look deeply enough. Poor leaders are typically those who are struggling because they lack the skills inherent to great leadership—and leadership skills are not what most people assume they are, as you will discover in the next chapter.

Unhealthy cultures are driven by poor leaders so when ineffective leaders are eliminated, either through effective training and coaching or through replacement, cultures invariably get healthier.

It is important to note that it is much less expensive to coach and/or train an ineffective leader who is open to personal development than to start all over by hiring another manager that may ultimately have similar challenges. Poor leaders are often diamonds in the rough and a little polishing can turn them into real gems. The first step is to determine where natural talents lie and where learned skills might actually be creating stress. Without this awareness a potential superstar, rather than shining, may simply burn out.

Misplaced Employees

Employee misplacement is a huge problem, even in organizations that are trying to find ways to work closely with their employees. The inability to properly place employees, especially effective leaders, using standard practices is the primary reason why good companies have not moved to *great* almost a decade after Jim Collins published the results of his research. Certainly the research provided sufficient proof of the financial benefit of putting the right people in the right seats, so even OZ organizations that are focused on the bottom line should be interested.

Managers waste endless hours and millions of dollars essentially trying to fit round pegs into square holes or trying to shape the pegs to fit the holes. It never works. Potentially good employees in the wrong positions can look inept, incompetent or unmotivated because they are working against their nature. Even fish, which are born swimmers, will tire if constantly forced to swim upstream and, once they tire, even they can look pretty ineffective.

Likewise, when employees are regularly doing tasks that tax their energy and patience, in time, even the most dedicated will burn out. Add emotional immaturity to that equation and you've got real problems. Even people who are relatively mature under normal circumstances, often become immature under stress, and continually swimming against the natural flow creates stress for everyone in time.

When emotionally mature employees are placed in jobs that compliment their natural strengths, they seem tireless. They can breeze through the same work as the poorly placed employee in a fraction of the time and enjoy every minute of it. They are more positive, more upbeat and, far more productive. Motivated employees can accomplish more than three or four average workers, so finding ways to ensure that employees are motivated and fully engaged makes a lot of sense, even when the focus is the bottom line.

Hiring and placing employees without any consideration of their natural attributes is an expensive mistake. There is no way an individual can effectively alter natural abilities enough to excel at the wrong kind of work, and employees that are under-performing are rarely, if ever, fully engaged.

A natural athlete, for example, with very little technical acumen is never going to be a whiz at computer programming. He may be able to learn the basics and perform the tasks to some level of competence, but he will never shine at it.

Conversely, an individual with natural technical intelligence, but minimal athletic abilities, will never be a star athlete. As in the first example, he may be able to learn enough skills to compete as an athlete, but he too will never be a star player. Reverse the roles of these two, however, and each of them will quickly shine in the area of his natural talent with a little training.

The same rule applies in the workplace. It is not uncommon to see people who have very little propensity for details occupying jobs such as bookkeeping, filing, data entry, editing and other positions that require a lot of attention to detail. Though they work very hard at getting it right, lots of costly mistakes occur.

Finding employees with natural technical or systems orientation, but little propensity to develop good people skills, in customer service positions, especially on help desks, is fairly common too. Many customers are lost at the hands of these individuals, who likely mean well, but really don't enjoy dealing with people (and it shows).

Another major contributor to employee problems is poor communication and lack of understanding between executives and their employees and this too is a factor of natural traits development. Those who typically occupy executive level positions tend to be direct, to the point types, and that's how they communicate, which often creates an arena where all kinds of misunderstanding occurs and where instructions can go horribly awry.

For today's workforce, the ideal organizational environment is very much like the ideal home environment. Each member is understood well enough to know what to expect and each member is valued as an individual, while still considering the good of the entire family.

The environment is neither too rigid nor too lax. There are clear rules and guidelines which the entire group considers to be fair, but there is also a certain flexibility that allows each member to contribute at his or her own current level of development, and there are provisions made to enhance the development of those who are not performing to their fullest potential.

Most organizations could benefit greatly by observing the dynamics of a healthy family and using that model to create an environment that feels more like a healthy home.

You don't need to be helped any longer.

You've always had the power to go back home.

Glinda, the Good Witch
From *The Wizard of Oz*

CHAPTER NINETEEN
The Visionary Leader

I love research projects so when *Good to Great* by Jim Collins came out, I was intrigued by the description of what Collins referred to as Level 5 Leaders. As the originator and codeveloper of the CORE line of assessments I was aware that the description pointed to leaders that would profile on the CORE MAP assessment system as well developed in at least two areas (trait sets) and as emotionally competent in at least three.

As a researcher, I decided to test my hypothesis so Gina, also a codeveloper of the CORE line of assessments and a master at interviewing, and I set out to find leaders that fit the Level 5 model. We have analyzed 38 people identified by peers, employees and associates as Level 5 leaders using the in-depth CORE MAP system combined with interviews.

That research is still on-going. Our goal is to locate at least 100 Visionary Leaders and gather profiles on each of them. Finding them is not an easy task though. That may be, in part, because there are too few of them, but we suspect the main reason is that they are too humble to climb to the top of a building and pound on their chests. They tend to stay under the radar. We found, as Jim Collins did, that the majority of Visionary Leaders are not well known and they are perfectly content with that fact. Most of them don't think they are doing anything unusual so don't see any reason to step into the limelight. But, whether they see it or not, they are most certainly doing something unusual and, based on our research, are quite different than the typical CEO or Chairman of the Board.

Because CORE MAP measures broader and deeper than other assessments we were able to see how well various traits were developed in these leaders as compared to the average leader, how they cope under stress, what attributes they call on to manage stress, what attributes they use on an average day and how they tend to use them.

What our research revealed is that Level 5 leaders, which we prefer to call Visionary Leaders, have very different profiles than those of leaders found in most organizations and very different traits than most organizations prize.

The most prized traits were certainly present in Visionary Leaders, but did not exist in the order or to the degree in which they are prized in typical organizations. On the other hand, traits often dismissed as unimportant or "too soft" or "squishy" in many organizations were well developed and often the most frequently used by Visionary Leaders.

Here are the leadership traits most organizations seek in the order of their importance:

Most Prized ("Commander" traits in the CORE system)

- The desire to get things done

- Achievement drive

- Willingness to lead

- Direct, to the point communications

- A take-charge assertive style

- Goal orientation

- Ability to see the big picture

- Problem-solving

- Decisiveness – the ability to make quick, firm decisions

- The ability to strategize well

- Willingness to meet challenges

- Cool-headedness in emergencies

- The ability to anticipate the future as it relates to things, work, and achievement

Second Most Prized ("Organizer" traits in the CORE system)

- The desire to get things right

- A serious, deliberate approach to work

- A sense of duty and responsibility to do a good job

- A sense of order, structure, precision and predictability

- A thorough, orderly, methodical or systematic approach

- The desire to finish what is started

- The ability to plan carefully and check plans

- Ability to work well within hierarchies

- A clear opinion of right and wrong

- Ability to analyze closely and attend to specifics - likes schedules, lists, charts, graphs, numbers

- Ability to analyze and consider what might go wrong

- Patience in dealing with details and procedures

- Attention to details as they relate to things, facts, figures

Third Most Prized ("Entertainer" traits in the CORE system)

- The desire and willingness to be highly visible

- Social ability

- Verbal acuity - ability to communicate one-on-one or in groups

- Boldness with people - uninhibited in connecting with others

- Ability to stimulate action and excitement

- Ability to keep things light, upbeat and interesting

- Charisma, charm, creativity and colorfulness

- Ability to influence and inspire others

- Spontaneous innovativeness

- Ability to enjoy play and be light-hearted

- Ability to multi-task

- Ability to lead others into new activities and adventures

- Ability to allow self to be as important as others

- The ability to anticipate the future as it relates to people, experience, and innovation

- The ability to trust feelings in an intuitive way

Least Prized ("Relater" traits in the CORE system)

- The desire to get along with others and to build and sustain long term relationships

- Thoughtfulness, consideration and loyalty to others

- Genuine empathy

- Conscientiousness and obedience

- Willingness to follow the lead of others as necessary

- Good listening and observational skills

- Flexibility and an easygoing attitude

- Patience and ease in relating to and accepting others

- Team cohesiveness

- Creating environments that promote harmony and balance

- Attention to details as they relate to people, aesthetics

- Willingness to mediate toward more harmonious relationships

- Acceptance of others

Notice that the order typically prized by organizations for leaders is Commander-Organizer-Entertainer-Relater

Though the Relater trait set is the one least prized in leaders, Entertainer behaviors are the ones most frequently discouraged in general in typical organizations. The Entertainer style is frequently viewed as too "out there," too spontaneous and too openly emotional. Yet this was either the dominant or secondary trait set for all but two of the Visionary Leaders in the study.

The typical order of development and use in Visionary Leaders is Commander-Entertainer-Relater-Organizer.

In examining the development levels of the four traits, Visionary Leaders had all four trait sets developed to healthy levels, but in 89% of the leaders in the study the trait set that is second most prized and promoted in organizations, Organizer, was the dormant or least preferred and least used style. In the few leaders where Organizer was not the dormant style, it was the tertiary or backup style in all but two, where it was the secondary style, but Entertainer and Relater were very well developed in these two leaders.

The Entertainer style, the value of which most organizations greatly discount, was almost tied with Commander, the most prized leadership trait set. The overall difference in development between the two styles was only 6%, and several of the Level 5 Visionary Leaders in the study led with Entertainer though, where this was the case, Commander was the secondary style and exerted a strong influence.

Visionary Leaders Have Heart

One striking trend among the Visionary Leaders was that most of them have very well developed preferences for the feeling function. Several leaders in the study, both male and female, led with feeling, and where the thinking function led, feeling was not far behind.

This flies in the face of everything most organizations believe makes a great leader. Organizations look for and push Commander "get it done" and Organizer "get it right" traits and behaviors. Both are logical, thinking, left-brain styles. Yet only two leaders in the study actually led with this combination. Organizer was almost always in the backup or dormant position.

It is apparently the combination of the Commander trait set and the "soft", "squishy" feeling styles, Entertainer and Relater, that creates the most effective leaders. Organizer is used effectively, to be sure, but only as a tool in most and only as necessary. Though Relater was the backup style of most of the Visionary Leaders, it was developed to healthy levels and humility, a Relater trait, was apparent in every leader studied. One leader led with Relater, but Commander was a well developed backup style.

One Dallas-based organization that participated in the study, TD Industries, had three leaders that were each identified as L5 Visionaries. Each was assessed and interviewed separately, and each one gave the other two most of the credit for the company's success. It was apparent that each genuinely held that opinion too. One of them described the leadership style of the three as being like geese which, when flying in formation take turns leading in order to reduce the stress and fatigue of being at the head of the formation. Each recognized and valued the strengths of the other and each was willing to step aside and let the others take the lead as required.

No leader with a big ego would willingly step aside and turn the organization over to someone else. Most won't even relinquish control of a department, much less an entire organization.

TD Industries has had the well earned honor of being on Fortune Magazine's list of the Best Companies to Work for in America every year since the inception of that prestigious award. These three great leaders turned the company into an employee-owned enterprise, much like Southwest Airlines, another Dallas-based company created by Visionary Leader, Herb Kelleher.

There is a palpable difference in the way organizations run by Visionary Leaders feel. When you walk into one you know this is a genuinely people-centered organization. They know what their most valuable asset is and they let it shine.

At TD Industries, the first thing you see when you enter the building is a huge wall of employee photographs, beautifully framed and proudly displayed. They are ordered by the length of employment. Most employees have been at TD Industries for more than ten years.

At Intuit, the maker of QuickBooks, TurboTax and other software, you walk into a lobby that is warm and inviting. There are rugs on the floor that proclaim the company's employees to be "Honest", "Smart", "Committed", "Spirited", and "Real." And you believe it. The employees believe it too and it shows. Everyone you meet proudly displays those qualities.

Wall hangings aren't just pretty pictures at Intuit. They are messages to all who enter the well designed facility located on beautiful campus-like grounds. The wall hangings say things like "Trust", "Integrity", "Innovate", "Listen", "Life", "Teams" and "People". And the company's philosophy around each of these words is explained.

Intuit has a reputation for excellence and very low employee turnover. Julie and I interviewed Intuit's HR Director Marc Underwood, as we were preparing to write this book to get some insight into what they were doing right. Here's what he shared:

- Leaders are held to a very high standard. First and foremost they must understand people.

- Leaders invest considerable time on employee development.

- They discuss how, why and what needs to be done and why it is important with their team.

- They encourage a significant amount of unstructured time for employees, and their healthy annual profits attest to the efficacy of this approach.

- They assess employee engagement levels annually and take a pulse mid-year, and have better than 90% voluntary employee participation in this program.

- They have a very diverse workforce and regular diversity training to help employees understand and appreciate one another.

- They actively hire and engage Gen X and Millennials and appreciate and utilize the current technical savvy they bring to the table. When it comes to technology, these individuals have a unique perspective and style that is accretive to the organization when pro-actively engaged.

- Leaders are taught to look at employees' humanity, not just at what they can do for the company.

- They believe they can deliver great outcomes by ensuring employees have a great place to work, and through customer driven innovation.

- To encourage and reward innovation, they allow for flexible work schedules where it makes sense, and they provide the right technology and support to ensure success. They don't worry about where, how or when the work gets done as long as it gets done well and on time.

What Intuit is doing works well. Intuit CEO, Brad Smith, is adamant about keeping things real and transparent. Clearly Intuit is NOT an OZ organization.

Not surprisingly, just about every Visionary led department or company we examined operates under a similar philosophy and follows a similar path. We believe these are the philosophies and methods to which every leader should aspire and which every company should seek to emulate because, with Generation X and Millennials, they are the only ones that work.

True Leadership

True leadership has been defined as the ability to persuade others to do things the way you want them done and *like it*. Visionary Leaders are masters at this. They have made it a point to discover exactly what will motivate, inspire, and persuade their employees to do their best, and they use that information to create win/win environments. The leader wins by getting the desired result and the employees win because they are doing something they enjoy in an environment that supports and enhances them.

As many leaders have discovered to their dismay, employees rarely give their all in a typical work setting where Theory X leadership reigns. On the other hand, employees regularly go above and beyond the call of duty under the leadership of a Visionary Leader.

Visionary Leaders across the board view people from a Theory Y perspective. They expect the best from their people and they regularly get it. They typically get 100% of their people's energy and commitment with very little need to continually monitor them and certainly without coercion. Healthy company profits prove the effectiveness of this style over and over again.

Glinda

As we have journeyed through the Land of Oz, we have described all the characters except one, Glinda the Good Witch of the North. We saved her for this chapter because Glinda represents the Visionary Leader.

Her role in the story of Oz was one of guide and advisor. She was there when she was needed, but kept her distance and allowed Dorothy and her companions plenty of room to develop their own strengths and abilities.

She kept an eye out and knew what they were doing at any given time, but she didn't step in and do for them what she was sure they could do for themselves. She was effective without being overbearing, and at no point did she place herself above those she sought to serve. The name, Glinda, can be used as a great acronym for Visionary Leadership: *Great Leaders Inspiring Natural Development Authentically.*

Great leaders understand the immense potential of people who are encouraged and inspired to develop their natural talents. So Visionary Leaders take the time to learn what their people need to develop to their highest potential and function at their best, and are fully invested in providing it.

Visionary Leaders don't delude themselves into thinking that trying to fit square pegs into round holes is a short cut to building an effective team. They know that misplaced people are unhappy and functioning far below their potential, so they make certain that they have the right people in the right seats. Even though it may take more time and effort up front to ensure that employees discover and develop their natural traits, they know that aligning task performance with natural traits is the only route to good job fit. They also know that good job fit will save worlds of time and effort in the long run, prevent many mistakes and keep employees happy and productive.

Visionary Leaders know that the only way to keep the best and brightest people is to show up authentically and create conditions that allow employees to function authentically as well.

True North

Interestingly, Glinda is the good witch of the North, which fits with the Visionary Leader's practice of developing "True North" values and competencies in themselves and their people. True North values are those that align with authenticity, and True North competencies are those that align with naturally preferred traits and abilities.

Authenticity in the workplace and an environment that encourages the use and development of natural talents don't just make for happy, productive workers either; they make the job of leadership much easier and substantially add to an organization's bottom line.

Need proof? Look at the financial track records of Fortune Magazine's *100 Best Companies to Work For.* They regularly outperform companies in similar markets and industries, sometimes by more than seven times!

Each of the companies Jim Collins presented in *Good to Great* demonstrate that even under-performing companies can make a dramatic turn-around under the guidance of a great leader. The companies in Collins' study increased their value by as much as 18.5 times under the right kind of leadership, and these were not just short term spikes either. Each of the companies Collins studied outperformed the market and sustained their impressive growth and profits over the fifteen years Collins tracked them.

It doesn't matter whether a company is consumer driven or industrial, offering products or services, in a crisis or steadily holding their own prior to a change from ordinary leadership to Visionary Leadership, once the change occurs the organization comes to life. Employees begin to breathe again. They learn to trust and productivity soars. Healthy profits are then not far behind.

When TD Industries was facing a severe financial crunch during the housing debacle of the eighties, the Visionary Leaders of that organization didn't start laying people off. They called them all together and told them the truth. Then they asked them to help and offered them a piece of the company pie if they pulled together and kept things going. Almost no one got scared and left. Instead, they all tightened their belts, took pay cuts and started cutting out every penny of waste. Many of the employees even invested their savings in the company. Where most construction-related organizations were suffering, TD Industries was getting stronger and better with every passing day. By the time the economy recovered they were thriving and they still are.

Pulling Together as a Team

What the companies thriving in today's economy have in common is not that they are downsizing to conserve money. It is that they are pulling together as a real team under the leadership of a true visionary.

Both our study and that of Jim Collins found that great leaders share the unusual combination Collins identified as "modest and willful, humble and fearless". Visionary Leaders can be modest and humble because they are comfortable enough with their position of power to give the credit for their great successes to their people. They are willful and fearless in that they are willing and able to make hard decisions and follow through on them.

One interesting trend in our study was the tendency for Visionary Leaders to show a slight degree of impatience around the need to get things done coupled with a great degree of patience in working with people.

One leader explained the trend: "I am very patient with people as long as they are performing as well I know they can. I expect them to be on top of their game and they usually are. But, to use a football analogy, when you are just one yard from the goal line and the team needs a swift kick to get them over that line, I am not opposed to delivering that kick. I know the team won't enjoy it in the moment, and neither do I, but I also know that when they are celebrating their victory, I'm the first guy they want to hug."

This is the "willful" factor which is expressed as having a clear vision and solid, non-negotiable values that guide every decision, and which are clearly communicated to the entire workforce and insisted upon at all times—no exceptions. Visionary Leaders are disciplined themselves and they maintain a disciplined, but healthy environment—much like that of the parents in the healthy home described in chapter eighteen.

The "fearless" factor is expressed as Visionary Leaders' willingness to admit that they don't have all the answers; that they are fallible and sometimes need help too. It is expressed in the willingness to learn and grow and consider new information even if it comes from the janitor; to invite the ideas of their people and to allow their own ideas to be as openly challenged as the ideas of employees in healthy debate.

When the employee is right, humility allows a Visionary Leader to accept that fact and apply the employee's solution. When the opinions or beliefs of employees are discovered, through debate or research, to be wrong fearlessness allows Visionary Leaders to move ahead in spite of prevailing opinions, and to "kick them over the goal line" if that is what it takes to ensure their people are performing to their highest potential.

Profile of a Visionary Leader

Because we used the CORE MAP analysis system in our study, we were able to see factors that were not visible to Collins in his study. The significant trends we uncovered were:

1. Commander as a dominant or secondary style, which was no surprise because Commander is the most prized trait set for leaders. Even in the rare instance that this style is not dominant or secondary, it is well developed in Visionary Leaders.

2. A coping pattern that reveals slight impatience around Commander. In interviews, leaders agreed that there was generally a sense of urgency around the primary Commander

need to get things done. Many explained it as purposefully maintaining a sense of urgency to make sure their people had what they needed when they needed it. That Visionary Leaders used this impatience to the benefit of their people and the company was reflected in the fact that overall Commander patterns were very healthy (well developed and non-reactionary).

3. Entertainer as a dominant or close secondary style, in spite of the fact that most organizations do not value Entertainer very highly and tend not to encourage this style.

4. Higher than expected feeling scores in males as well as females. Feeling is generally discouraged in the world of business. We frequently see the feeling function suppressed in the profiles of corporate leaders, especially when the leader is under stress. Apparently, Visionary Leaders have not bought into the "don't bring your feelings to work" mentality. Their effective use of feeling is a primary factor in their overall success as a leader.

5. The healthy development and frequent use of positive Relater traits in dealing with their people, though Relater was almost never used as a coping mechanism in stressful situations.

6. The tendency for Organizer traits to be the least preferred and least utilized, except for initial planning and coping with crises, in spite of the fact that this trait set is highly prized in most organizations.

7. The odd combination of slight impatience around getting things done (Commander) coupled with high empathy and patience with people (Relater). This dichotomy was generally explained as resulting from a sense of urgency in accomplishing desired outcomes combined with great faith in the people the leader has placed in charge of the task.

8. The tendency to consider personal wants and needs last when under stress. The leaders in the study were focused on the well-being of their people and on getting the result with almost equal intensity. Many stated that they placed very little attention on self in a crisis because *self* was the best understood and most predictable part of the equation.

9. A high degree of concern for the well-being of their people.

10. Exceptional interpersonal skills. Visionary Leaders show great ease in connecting with people at any level and under almost any circumstance. An ability conferred by the healthy development of the Entertainer and Relater trait sets.

11. A different focus on challenges. Over the years Gina and I have interviewed thousands of managers and asked them to name the source of their greatest challenge. Ninety-eight percent of ordinary leaders name employees. Great leaders rarely do. Visionary Leaders tend to name the challenges their people face and their own feelings of inadequacy when they are unable to help their people meet those challenges. Visionary Leaders see their employees as their greatest asset. They expect great things from them and actively look for ways to bring out their best. Their sense of challenge is in finding effective ways to help their people be their best and understanding each of them well enough to lead them effectively.

12. Effective development of all four trait sets, with Organizer being the least preferred and least developed in 89% of the study group.

13. Like Collins, we found that Visionary Leaders were ever open to learning and growing. They don't look at problems and assume they exist because their people are not trained well enough. They look at themselves and question what they need to learn to be a more effective leader. Visionary Leaders advocate continuous improvement and constantly invest in it for themselves and their employees.

14. Unlike ordinary leaders, Visionary Leaders regularly get feedback from their employees to discover what they want and need to improve themselves and get the best outcomes. They do not make assumptions that can, and in typical organizations often do, prove costly.

The Feeling Factor

Visionary Leaders lead with heart as well as with intellect and logic, and they do it *in spite of* the prevailing corporate culture, not because of it. Most Visionary Leaders report that they learned their leadership style from great parents or a special teacher or mentor. Most corporations push logic and discourage feelings, but Visionary Leaders know that they cannot connect with people through logic and they want to connect with the people they lead. They know that showing their people that they genuinely care about them and trust them to be amazing is the only way to have dedicated people regularly performing amazing feats.

An example of this is the CEO of Intuit. He is known throughout the company for his ability to connect with his people at deep, meaningful levels. Employees describe him as a very charismatic man that really listens to employees. He is further described as a very honest and transparent man and as a leader that inspires those same qualities in his people.

Visionary Leaders tend to be masters at communication. This is partly due to the high influence of the Entertainer trait set and of developed Relater traits, both of which confer exceptional interpersonal skills. The other part is the high degree of emotional intelligence seen in the effectiveness patterns of Visionary Leaders.

Feelings in the Workplace

Entertainer and Relater, two of the three best developed trait sets seen in Visionary Leaders, are products of the feeling function. Entertainer confers excellent communication and connection skills when developed effectively. Relater, when developed effectively, confers excellent relationship building and listening skills, and genuine empathy. The two in combination result in exceptional interpersonal skills.

Most great orators and, as it turns out, most great leaders, have well developed Entertainer traits. Entertainers have the natural ability to be eloquent and charismatic speakers and when this trait set is developed effectively, they usually are. They connect with people easily and have a natural enthusiasm that is genuinely inspiring.

Organizations need leaders who have the feeling functions developed to healthy levels, but few do anything to make that happen. Most organizations actually discourage feeling in the workplace because they mistakenly believe feelings are messy. The reality is, feelings are only messy when they have been suppressed too long and are released only when stress gets too high to contain them. Feelings expressed in healthy ways almost always unite people and inspire them to greater performance.

If you want to know how feelings affect people when they are allowed to express in healthy ways, just go find a Visionary Leader and talk with him or her for a few minutes. Then talk to that leader's people. You will come away from the experience transformed, not just in mind, but in spirit.

CHAPTER TWENTY
Transforming OZ: A New Emerald City

In the end, Dorothy and her companions came to understand that the Great Oz had none of the answers they sought; in fact, they discovered he wasn't even a wizard. He was just an ordinary man trying to maintain an impossibly difficult illusion

What Dorothy finally learned was that what she and her companions set out to find was already theirs and had been available to them all along.

The "Great Oz" who initially sought to control Dorothy and her friends through fear, intimidation, and threats turned out to be a decent guy once they managed to get past his façade and force him to get real. Because Dorothy and her friends exposed his truth, the "wizard" was finally able to drop the long maintained pretense. Had he not, the ruse would have continued and the kindly old man would have been stuck in the difficult to maintain role he had created; a role that required him to live a fear-filled inauthentic life separated from his people, from enjoyment, and from life itself.

This is essentially what will soon be happening in OZ organizations around the world. Generation X and the Millennials are busily exposing Wizards and, while it is uncomfortable and downright scary to the Wizards right now, in the long run many of them will discover, to their delight, that they then have the opportunity to reinvent themselves in wonderfully authentic (and effective) ways.

The Makings of a Visionary Leader

Gina and I have been collecting leader profiles for fifteen years and have thousands of them in our CORE database. Because CORE MAP looks deeply and broadly enough to see natural tendencies, as well as how effectively those tendencies have been developed and are being utilized, we can see that 94% of the people in leadership roles (mid-management and above) have the makings of a Visionary Leader. The traits are not effectively developed in most, but they are there. What we often find is that Commander traits are somewhat reactionary, Organizer traits are highly reactionary, and Relater and Entertainer traits are suppressed.

We know from years of working with people that under the right conditions, natural traits can easily, and often quickly, be developed because nature itself steps in and assists in the development when given the right catalyst.

Most ineffective leaders are not ineffective because they don't *have* the right stuff. They are ineffective because they have not *developed* the right stuff.

Many leaders in OZ organizations would love to be Level 5 Visionary Leaders, and most are capable of it. They just don't know where to begin. The pomp and ceremony and all the expectations pushed upon them have prevented them from developing to healthy levels. The feeling functions, so critical to Visionary Leadership, have been discouraged and suppressed for so long that they have forgotten how to access them and, without the benefit of the feeling functions, they continue to struggle to lead people they cannot connect with and who cannot connect with them.

The Freeing Effect of Exposure

It's interesting how exposure tends to change people. Exposure, like a near death experience, takes us to our most vulnerable place. Where a near death experience can make us more aware of the value of life, exposure can make us more aware of the value of authenticity.

At first people are appalled at being exposed. They are embarrassed and ashamed. They hit an emotional bottom and then, for most, something amazing happens. They realize that they can't get any lower emotionally than they already are and decide to explore new options. They re-evaluate who they have been and who they want to be now.

With nothing left to hide, they discover they are *free*. They can accept the consequences of their previous actions, then leave them behind and start all over. They can write a brand new chapter in their life—a more authentic chapter—a more loving, connected, worthwhile chapter.

Some OZ leaders, seeing this coming, will choose to step from behind the curtain on their own. Others will have to suffer the humiliation of involuntary exposure. Those who choose to reveal themselves will, with sufficient training and insights, become Visionary Leaders. Those who continue to hide are not likely to because their egos won't allow it.

But change is coming to the world of work and it is going to be substantial. Organizations are already seeing the effects of this change, but they haven't seen anything yet.

To be prepared and to survive and thrive through this sea-change, leaders will need to re-examine themselves and their assumptions. They will need to deeply understand the new workforce so they are able to get the best from these new generations and, to do that, they will need to transform the workplace.

To gain some perspective on the direction in which transformation will need to go, a look at the new workforce will be helpful.

There's a New World Coming

In the past, employees stayed with a job until the pain of staying exceeded the expected pain of leaving. To manage employee retention in the past all that was necessary was to lower the pain of staying a little. That philosophy will not work with the new workforce.

Every generation is strongly shaped by their circumstances and life situations, and Generation X and Millennials are no exception. Because these generations grew up in uncertain times, the uncertainty of not having a job is not as painful to them as it was to earlier generations.

The stigma of holding multiple jobs is not a factor for these generations either. And they don't have a false sense of loyalty. Leaders will have to earn the loyalty of these generations. Once earned, Generation X and especially Millennials can be fiercely loyal, but they don't give loyalty or trust easily. They saw what happened to their Traditional grandparents and their Baby Boomer parents, who were loyal to companies that were not loyal in return.

The hard, cold fact, and one many OZ leaders don't warm up to very well, is that the new workforce is *radically different* than previous generations.

Always before, employers have been able to mold employees to fit the organization. That was before the internet, social media, endless access to information, wi-fi, iPods and cell phones. In this hi-tech, well informed, highly mobile world it is the *employer* that must change, because today's workforce is not about to.

They are a whole new breed, built from a completely different set of life experiences and governed by a whole new set of values. For companies to survive and thrive in today's quickly changing global marketplace, they *must* adapt. The massive hemorrhaging of profits has already begun in traditional organizations and will continue right up to their painful death if they fail to adjust.

Another factor that will drive this sea-change is that the workforce is shrinking. Soon the demand for employees will exceed the qualified labor pool. This is pretty common knowledge, so it's safe to assume Generation X and Millennials are aware of it. They are also aware that, in a shrinking labor pool, they have a lot of options and they will be quick to exercise them.

By 2020 the workforce will be almost completely dominated by Generation X and Millennials. To survive in this new world, OZ leaders must let go of the old rules and create something brand new.

So how does OZ transform? It won't be easy, but critical shifts in the marketplace or in the workforce usually require radical change if an organization is to remain viable.

Whitewashing staid old organizations and calling them new and improved will not work. Platitudes about being people-centric will not work either. OZ leaders are quite good at fooling themselves about such things, but the people are not buying. Serious change will need to occur at the very *core* of the organization, beginning with its values, and spreading throughout.

Values Alignment

All organizations have core values which need to align with the organization's vision and mission, and also to the values of the workforce. That was not so hard to do with previous generations, even Baby Boomers, because they were taught by Traditional parents to honor the traditional workplace. Not so for Generation X and Millennials.

Baby Boomers followed traditional teachings, but they didn't necessarily agree with them so didn't teach them to their children. Values are radically different for Generation X and especially for Millennials than for previous generations, so organizations will have to make some radical changes to align company values with the values held by the new workforce.

Corporate leaders can no longer dictate corporate values and expect employees to follow them. To get buy-in from the new generations, organizations will need to allow the workforce to help shape the values of the organization the way they were allowed to help shape life at home. This will not sit well with many organizations, but ultimately it will prove to be a good move.

More than eighteen years ago John P. Kotter and James L. Heskett presented a study that showed a strong correlation between companies with strong adaptive cultures based on shared company/employee values and profitability. Values-aligned companies outperformed other companies by a significant margin.

The study, conducted over an eleven-year period, found that companies that considered the values of all stakeholders, including employees, and aligned with these values, grew 4 times faster than companies that did not. The study also found that job creation rates for these companies were seven times higher. Stock prices grew 12 times faster and profit performance was 750 times higher than companies that did not have shared values and adaptive cultures (Kotter and Heskett, 1992).

In 2002 the majority of employees in large American corporations reported that the values of the company they worked for did not match their values, and the percentage of employees that hold that view is increasing as more Gen Xers and Millennials enter the workforce. Understanding the values of the emerging workforce and considering ways to align company values with them before it becomes a necessity would be a wise move.

Core Values of Generation X and Millennials

- Independence

- Self-reliance (these generatrions are not intimidated or overly influenced by authority)

- Adaptability

- Sociability

- Flexibility

- Team orientation (as a social or collaborative function rather than as a job function)

- Heroism (more true of Millennials than Gen Xers)

- Collaboration

- Informality

- Tolerance (as long as their values are not compromised)

- Work/Life Balance

Interestingly, these values closely match those held by some of the world's most successful people, which may be one of the reasons why organizations that align their values with those of the newer generations are prospering.

With such strong evidence for a correlation between the values of the newer generations and top performers, and a clear correlation between top performers and monetary gain, one would think that OZ organizations would be quick to integrate these values into their culture if for no other reason than to attract and keep talented workers. For some reason most have not.

Though most organizations invest a lot of time and money attracting talent, many don't know what to do with the new generations once they have them. They keep trying to fit them into the old management models and they just won't go, which is likely why OZ organizations are still delaying the inevitable.

Organizations that have built the values of these new generations into their culture are thriving even in a difficult economy—think Google.

Adhering to old corporate values is not profitable now and it sure won't be profitable in the future. The old established organizations move notoriously slow and, since they only have ten to twelve years to get it right, those who want to continue to exist need to get to work on this *now*.

Although there are, for the first time in history, four generations in the workplace today, all working from different perspectives and values, it is Generation X and Millennials that will determine the course of business over the next forty to fifty years. They currently make up almost 60% of the workforce and are steadily replacing the older generations.

Millennials, born between 1981 and 2002, along with the last quarter of Gen Xers, are a part of the largest generation since Baby Boomers. Most of this large group were born during what demographers have dubbed a "baby bulge", which occurred between 1979 and 1994. At 60 million strong, this group is more than three times the size of Generation X and not far behind Baby Boomers at 72 million. By 2020 this group will dominate the workplace.

The Four Generation Workplace

A brief overview of how all four generations function within the workplace might be useful in helping leaders understand what they need to be doing to prepare to succeed with the new workforce.

Based on what we continually hear from both company leaders and the new generations, there currently exists a huge gap between the majority of leaders, most of whom belong to the Post-World War II and Baby Boom generations, and the workforce, the majority of whom belong to the Generation X and Millennial generations. To bridge that gap, every generation needs to better understand and appreciate the others.

Traditionals

The oldest workers in today's workplace were born between 1935 and 1945. These are the last of the Traditionals, sometimes called the Silent Generation, the Lost Generation or the Post War Generation. The values this generation brings to the workplace are products of parents and teachers who lived through the Great Depression and World War II. At the hands of challenge-hardened adults they learned the value of hard work and sacrifice; values they expect from themselves and tend to expect from others. They are now in their mid-sixties and older. Executives and upper level managers that belong to this generation will soon be retiring.

Baby Boomers

The Baby Boom generation, born between 1946 and 1964, are now in their mid-forties to early sixties. They grew up during the fifties and sixties when life was relatively easy and carefree. Carefree living gave them the leisure to consider their own wants and needs and the Vietnam War, desegregation and the Women's Rights Movement gave them reasons to learn to express their opinions.

Baby Boomers don't value hard work and sacrifice the way the generation before them did, though they still have a strong work ethic and feel a duty to put in a full measure of time—and then some. But, because they also tend to value individuality and autonomy, many of them take a laissez-faire approach to leadership. It isn't that Boomer leaders are lazy. They most certainly are not. They just value freedom and autonomy and, in their mind, a hands-off approach is the best way to manage people.

Though the laissez-faire approach defined their parenting style as well as their leadership style and produced the "whatever" mindset of the younger generations, Baby Boomers in the workplace tend to have a problem with Gen Xers and Millennials because these generations don't buy into the idea of personal sacrifice that the Boomers bought from the Silent Generation. The newer generations don't respond well to the non-collaborative environments created by laissez-faire leadership. Baby Boomer leaders are frustrated because they are trying to give the "youngsters" the freedom to make their own choices, but the choices they are making are not the ones the Boomers expect. Boomers *expect* dedicated effort. What they *get* is what they see as lack of commitment and non-engagement. Why? Because the Gen Xers and Millennials expect collaboration and interpret the hands-off leadership style as lack of commitment on the part of the leader.

Generation X and Millennials

Generation X, born between 1965 and 1980, are now in their late twenties to mid-forties so they will remain in the workforce for twenty to forty years. Millennials will be in the workforce for the next fifty years or more. These generations understand the meaning and application of personal power like no generations before them. They are dedicated to building a purposeful lifestyle and don't buy into the "duty first" mantra. The strong value of a worthwhile life is what drives their decision to simply leave a job that does not support that goal.

It is not uncommon to hear leaders complaining that these generations don't even wait for the end of the week or pay period to leave a job. They are just as likely to leave right in the middle of a shift if things get too stressful. This is a big problem that is just going to get bigger until leaders adopt a new, more collaborative and more empowering leadership style.

Rather than being willing to make sacrifices to keep a job, these generations make sacrifices to ensure that they can live life on their own terms. They want a collaborative environment and actively seek ways to create one. Their attempts to build collaboration in dysfunctional environments is often viewed by leadership as socializing or goofing off, and indeed it can turn into that where environments do not support true collaboration.

Learning to get the best from Generation X and Millennials may seem distasteful to leaders with different values, but the reality is that the two older generations are rapidly declining in the workforce and the two younger ones are rapidly increasing. The "problems" their values create are not going away. Rather than chafing at them, it makes a lot more sense to begin learning how to adjust, and there are lots of ways to do that without undue stress. Let's examine a few.

Empowerment

Empower employees to work more independently. This does not mean being lax or using a laissez-faire leadership style, quite the contrary. Empowerment is an organizational process, embedded into the very nature of a company's culture, that allows and encourages employees to independently take action, make decisions and control outcomes regarding their own work within clearly defined boundaries that are adhered to consistently.

Since empowered employees are as much as 400% more effective and take up 80% less of their manager's time, leaders should be clamoring to empower independent workers. But the idea of an independent, self-directed workforce is positively frightening to OZ leaders. It would be a death knell to the Wizard's brand of power and control. Yet, without empowerment, employee engagement is just a pipe dream when it comes to the new workforce and without engagement, organizations can forget about performance.

Engagement

Engagement is defined as the positive emotional connection employees feel toward their employer, and their resultant willingness to put forth greater effort on the employer's behalf.

Engagement is a by-product of employers and employees trusting each other, and trust is not a condition generally found in OZ organizations. In the absence of company-wide trust, employee engagement is very low, but can still be found in organizations where employees find their work stimulating, can see how their efforts fit into the overall success of the company, and where their leader and the immediate environment support their aspirations.

In OZ organizations, engaged employees, if any exist, are typically found in isolated departments run by Visionary Leaders that encourage, empower and fiercely protect their people from the overall environment.

Most people seek a sense of pride and positive self-esteem. These are primary human motivators. Employers that provide an environment where personal pride and self-esteem flourish can create a dedicated team no matter what generation the employees are from, and often no matter what the rest of the organization is doing. It requires building company pride as well as team and individual pride however, and company pride is not always possible in OZ organizations.

Wherever there is a discrepancy between an employee's self-image and the image of the company (or the image the company has of employees), the employee will disengage and eventually leave.

If, for example, an employee sees himself as honest, trustworthy and a person of integrity, and the company acts in a way that seems dishonest, or lacking in trust and integrity, there is an immediate disconnect and the employee emotionally steps away from the relationship and disengages. From that point forward, the employee tends to give to the employer minimal effort (average at best), but never their best.

Engaged employees are more innovative, more productive, and more committed to customer satisfaction than their less engaged peers. They are far more effective and produce more profits for their organization than their less engaged peers. This is not speculation, there is good research and hard data that supports this and anyone can access it. Most leaders are regularly exposed to such statistics so the big question is, why are there any leaders left that are not working toward building an organizational culture that fosters employee engagement? We find there are typically two reasons:

1. They don't know how or

2. They are focused on power rather than profits.

Performance

Productive organizations have a similar set of characteristics. First, they have a culture of performance where company and employee values are aligned. Performance-based organizations are *results* focused. They don't care how much or how little time an employee spends on a project or how they go about getting the job done as long as the job gets done well and on time. And there are effective systems in place in performance-based organizations to ensure that there is a good fit between the job and the employee.

Generation X and Millennials love performance-based workplaces because they fit their model of how things should be. They see no wisdom in clocking eight hours a day, five days a week to amass a forty hour week when it isn't necessary to get the job done.

Organizations should love performance-based work too, but many don't have a clear enough idea of what is required for the effective completion of the many projects being juggled at any given time to know how to measure performance. They cling to the time-based model because they know how to measure time spent on a project, but are not so clear on what constitutes performance.

Time spent is certainly no measure of performance, but most organizations continue to use that model because they falsely believe that captive employees will get more done than those who are free to perform in their own way.

Recall the research we conducted over several years and in multiple organizations where employees reported wasting as much as four hours a day—the *employees,* not their managers. That most were frustrated by that fact speaks volumes for the potential and profitability that is lost in organizations every day.

Studies repeatedly show that the vast majority of people hate putting in time that feels unproductive. Most employees want to be rewarded for good performance, not for the dutiful serving of time. This is especially true of the new workforce. They want the opportunity to prove their worth and then be trusted to complete clearly defined projects in their own way.

If they complete the day's projects in five hours, they want to be free to leave work and do whatever they please. If they complete the week's projects in four days, they want the freedom to stay home on the fifth day without having to make up some excuse for it. Time off is a meaningful perk that keeps today's generations motivated to perform at peak levels.

Not all jobs lend themselves to such flexibility, and many leaders worry that employees who need to be on the job during business hours will resent those who can leave at the end of a project. Perhaps they will. But even so, is it better to have a few resentful employees or a whole bunch of them?

The solution is simple really. All that is necessary is for a company to explain their performance-based policies to incoming employees so the ones who accept jobs that require their presence all day know, going in, that project-based employees are not bound by hours. If this is made clear from the beginning, resentment is not nearly as likely to crop up. It all boils down to communication and transparency—something sorely lacking in OZ organizations.

Visionary Leadership

Another characteristic of productive organizations is that they are adamant about having effective leaders. They have legitimate feedback mechanisms in place and are quick to retrain, redirect or remove any and all employees who fall short of the very high standards they set. All employees are held to high standards, but this is especially so for their leaders.

One of the many things productive organizations expect in their leaders is vision—the ability to look beyond the obvious and see possibilities. Visionary Leaders do that quite naturally.

Walt Disney was a Visionary Leader and used that quality to build an empire from nothing but imagination. The companies he founded still rely on standards set by his vision.

An example is the practice of "plus it" where employees are given a project and directed to brainstorm it to come up with the best ideas the team can generate. Once everyone agrees that they have all the ideas they can generate, they collectively choose the best from among them.

Once they settle on the best idea and determine the specifics of what it will take to pull it off, the project leader goes back to the team and asks, "Now, how can we plus it?" Very frequently someone comes up with an even better way. Imagine what could happen if every organization took this dynamic, visionary approach.

Trust

In his excellent book, *The Speed of Trust*, Stephen M. R. Covey states that trust is the "critical leadership competency of this new economy."

He makes a good case for the fact that, where trust is low, cost is high and, where trust is high, cost is low.

In low trust environments people are suspicious and vigilant about what they do. As vigilance goes up, speed goes down and, as speed goes down, costs go up. Conversely, in high trust environments confidence is high and vigilance low, so speed goes up and costs go down.

Now, the skeptic will typically object at this point that lack of vigilance and increased speed are likely to increase the error rate, driving costs up. But in an environment where there is mutual and authentic trust, the trust is well earned not arbitrarily given. Each individual knows the capabilities of the other so expectations are never unrealistic and trust is never applied in a haphazard way.

Diligence is what prevents mistakes, not vigilance, and diligence—steady, earnest, energetic effort—is a product of trust. Genuine trust never results in an increase in mistakes. As Covey so aptly puts it, "trust is always a dividend and distrust always a tax" (Covey 2006).

But how do organizations get to a place of authentic trust? The first step requires leaders to tear down those curtains, toss out the smoke machines and trick mirrors, step out of their fortress and connect with their people in a genuine way. Only then can trust begin to develop.

For many that is a very frightening thought, but it need not be. With the right training and coaching most leaders can successfully make that transition. The only prerequisite is to get egotism (which is always based in fear) out of the way and adopt the kind of humility typically seen in truly great leaders. Once a leader is open to learning, real magic can occur and it doesn't take smoke and mirrors to pull it off.

Communication

It is not possible to genuinely connect with people in a meaningful way without good communication skills. Communication is not just a way with words as many believe. That is just part of the package. But, just as good tires for a car do not translate to reliable transportation, neither do words alone translate to genuine communication. Like good tires on a vehicle, they can make the "ride" smoother, but words in and of themselves won't get you very far.

Communication is both verbal and non-verbal. It is both attitude and application. It is the ability to listen and hear not just what is being said, but what is *not* being said. It is the ability to see past awkward silences and reach for the truth in a way that allows it to be spoken.

Effective communication is a two way street in more ways than most imagine. We are all aware that there needs to be a two-way process to have a conversation, but few recognize the depth of the two-way process that generates an authentic connection.

To "get real", we must first know what "real" is for us, for the environments we navigate on a regular basis, and for the people that populate those environments. The first requirement for authentically connecting with others is to be authentic ourselves, and we cannot do that if we are not clear about who we are and where we stand.

In studying and assessing leaders over the years, both the visionary and the vain, it has become clear that Visionary Leaders are well acquainted with themselves and really do like who they are. Since they like what they see in the mirror, they don't feel they have anything to prove or hide, so authenticity and transparency are natural ways of being.

Those who are creating all kinds of discomfort for their unfortunate followers don't really know who they are, and usually don't much like the self they see. The two (don't know and don't like) are synonymous. People who know who they are authentically, and who have chosen to be authentic, always like who they are. The authors have more than ninety years of collective experience studying and assessing thousands of people and not one of us has ever seen a single exception.

Difficult people are stressed people. The stress may or may not come from the current environment. It might have begun way back in early childhood, but whatever the cause, stress produces discomfort and when discomfort is one's experience, that is what gets shared with others.

What does all this have to do with effective communication? *Everything.* Because the most vital form of communication; the form that impacts every attitude and ultimately every action and interaction, is *self*-communication; what we tell ourselves about who we are and what we capable of.

You Can't Take the Ass Out of Assumptions

Like a stubborn pack-mule on an expedition, few things can slow the realization of a goal faster than unfounded assumptions. They create all kinds of havoc when they are made without getting sufficient feedback to qualify them. This happens in hiring, placement, promotions and in giving directives.

For example, a boss hands off a project, a proposal designed to win over an important new client, to an employee that generally demonstrates effectiveness. The communication to the employee is "this could be a very big client so the proposal needs to be impressive. They need it by the end of the week. Can you get me a really great proposal by Wednesday so I will have time to review it?" The employee assures the boss it can be done and immediately goes to work on it. However, "impressive" to the employee means nice formatting and colorful illustrations (visual appeal), where "impressive" to the boss means lots of factual information with research references to qualify each point. What the boss gets on Wednesday is nowhere near what was expected and the hard work and dedication of the employee results not in praise, but disappointment. Now both the boss and the dedicated employee scramble and work overtime to try to get the project done on time, and it falls short of expectations for both of them.

Without continual feedback from employees, leaders can, and frequently do, create problems they never intended and never saw coming. It is not uncommon for employers to lament that they can't hand off projects without micromanaging them because employees rarely produce the intended results.

Sometimes this happens as a result of what Dr. Laurence J. Peter called "the Peter Principle" in his book of the same name, which states that in a hierarchy employees tend to get promoted to the level of incompetence, but that is not generally the cause or poor results. The more common cause is unqualified assumptions. In organizations where "incompetence" is a regular issue, one of the first things an employer should check is his or her own assumptions.

Hiring Mistakes

An example of how employers make hiring mistakes by not checking assumptions is Matt, the owner of a multi-office travel agency who sought help in fixing a problem with a valued employee. Matt had promoted the employee, Andrea, to management fifteen months earlier. He reported that she had been an excellent employee for seventeen years prior to the promotion so he assumed she would flourish as a branch manager.

Instead of flourishing however, within just a few months of being promoted Andrea grew "testy" and sullen. Other employees began complaining about her management style and it didn't take long for Matt to see that their complaints were legitimate. Andrea had become "a wet blanket" negatively impacting the entire division. Matt couldn't understand what had happened to this once positive and highly effective employee, but knew something had to be done to stem the ever growing problem. He confided that he felt Andrea's behavioral change was his fault somehow, but he didn't know exactly how.

A CORE MAP analysis of Andrea revealed that while she enjoyed working with people, she was very uncomfortable in a leadership role. She wanted desperately to please her boss however, so she was giving the new position all she had in spite of the extreme stress it was creating for her. The negative behaviors were a manifestation of Andrea's high stress levels and her mounting frustration at the fact that she was not as competent in this new position as she had been in her previous one and, as she put it, couldn't will herself to do better.

Matt very much wanted to keep Andrea in his employ so, upon my recommendation he gave her the option of moving back to her old position without taking a pay cut provided she assist whoever replaced her as manager. She happily and with great relief accepted the offer and moved to assistant manager role and resumed the work she had been doing for seventeen years with just a slight twist that she could easily manage.

Using the *CORE Personal Effectiveness Profile* (CORE PEP) my company screened those being considered for the management position and found an employee Matt already had at another branch that appeared to be perfect for the position. Andrea and the new manager hit it off beautifully and in a few weeks Andrea was back to her old, kind, reliable, productive self. Four years later she and the manager that replaced her are working together wonderfully and Andrea is still a valued employee. Had Matt not learned about Andrea's nature and needs, and had he not provided an avenue for her to move back toward them, he would have lost one of his best people.

Many managers, once they become aware of human nature and the many ways it impacts behaviors and interactions, report that they realize in hindsight that they have lost valuable employees by promoting them to positions for which they were unsuited, or by unknowingly mismanaging them.

The reason the Peter Principle is alive and well in many organizations is because people are hired and promoted based on unfounded assumptions. Visionary Leaders take the time to look deeply, ask pertinent questions and listen to minimize hiring mistakes. And like

Matt, they are quick to correct mistakes when they see they have been made.

Performance Mistakes

Assuming that employees can't or just don't follow orders well is a very common form of dysfunction among ordinary leaders. What prevents so many employers from solving this common problem is assuming that the *employees* are the problem when directives are not carried out properly. It is an assumption that frequently results in poor performance, bottlenecks and multiple failed projects, and that cost organizations billions of dollars every year.

This costly mistake occurs when managers look in the wrong direction when trying to fix performance problems. As long as employers continue to assume that employees "just don't get it" the problem is unsolvable. Most performance mistakes occur because assumptions are made and communications are ineffective. And whether miscommunication occurs because the employee is not listening or because the leader is not conveying the message well, it is always the leader's responsibility to ensure that effective communication has occurred.

The typical communication style of those in leadership positions is often at the heart of poor performance. Most leaders are generalists, meaning they tend to communicate in broad, non-specific terms. Though many know that non-specific directives yield very poor results, most generalists are not aware that they are giving directives too generally and are conveying impatience with the questions employees ask in an attempt to get specific details.

The tendency of most leaders is to start communications at "Z"—that is, with the goal or outcome they want. They then lay out a general outline of the direction in which they see the project going and expect the employees receiving the information to fill in the details. Problems occur when the employee receiving the instructions has different ideas as to what should fill all those holes left by the leader, or when they need to start at "A" (the first step of a process) and work systematically through the steps.

Because generalist leaders don't like dwelling on the specifics, they rarely provide enough details for employees to gather the information they need to go from step to step confidently and effectively. So while the manager is talking about "Z", the employee is generally back at "A" trying to figure out how to get to "B" and wondering what the manager actually wants.

When a leader doesn't offer or ask for feedback, employees tend not to ask for or offer any either. Sometimes they don't ask because they don't want to look dumb or incompetent, and sometimes because they have experienced or observed that the generalist leader gets irritated or impatient with their questions.

In either case, the employee just goes to work with fuzzy instructions hoping they can fill in all the holes effectively (I call this hole-filled style Swiss Cheese Communication for obvious reasons). The employee is left to assume what should go in all the holes and often they assume wrong. The leader then assumes that the employee is incompetent and the problems continue to escalate.

This is such a common occurrence between upper level managers and technical departments that almost everyone has heard a leader lament that the "techies just don't get it" or heard a "techie" make a similar comment about management. This wide divide is largely the result of failure on the part of management to know their people and communicate with them in the way they best understand.

Leaders tend to *like* the holes they leave in their communications, believing the holes leave room for creativity and innovation. But employees, trying to get clear on exactly what the leader wants, fear the holes and seek to fill them. This is especially true of introverted employees or those that are unsure of themselves. The fact that the leader is looking at the "cheese" and *likes* the holes, and the employee sees only the holes and fears them, is the cause of many misunderstandings and poorly completed projects.

Most organizations are full of good people longing to do a good job. When they are disengaged and unmotivated, it is not because they don't care, but because they are in a job or environment that does not support and sustain them.

To Get the Most from Employees:

1. Create a culture of open and complete communication to build understanding and engagement.

2. Spend the necessary resources to ensure the right job fit. There are three critical factors for sustained high performance and job fit is one of them. Understand the requirements of the job and the attributes necessary for non-resistance to task performance. Where there is resistance, there is energy drain and where there is energy drain, there is disengagement. Look deeply and broadly enough to know

exactly what you are getting, not just from a surface, self-reported perspective, but from deep, often unexplored core depths.

3. Align the company's core values with those of the workforce.

4. Increase emotional intelligence (EQ) as a core competency, particularly in leaders. Empathy is a social component of EQ and empathy increases trust. Studies show that high EQ is actually more important than high IQ for leaders.

5. Allow and encourage risk-taking. Convey that mistakes will not be penalized unless repeated. Clearly convey the consequences of repeated mistakes and follow through on them consistently. Also, regularly reward those who learn from mistakes and don't repeat them.

6. Create a team environment where everyone understands and accepts their individual and collective roles and responsibilities.

7. Build a solutions-without-boundaries environment; that is, create an atmosphere where good ideas and solutions can and do come from every level of the organization.

8. Provide training that aligns with interests.

Twelve Things Leaders Can Do Now to Attract and Retain Top Talent:

1. Know your employees and treat each one with the same degree of dignity and respect you want for yourself. Each employee is unique. Treat them as such.

2. Clearly communicate expectations, goals and rules. Be sure every employee knows what is expected and be very consistent with enforcement. What applies to one should apply to all.

3. Be sure you have the right people in the right seats. When you put your people in places and situations where they can succeed, they *will* succeed.

4. Give and ask for complete and honest feedback.

5. Actively listen – with your head *and* your heart.

6. Make the workplace fun. Celebrate successes both large and small.

7. Get employees involved and keep them informed. Let them know where they and the company stand and how their work fits into the overall company goals and mission.

8. Let employees know how they are doing and convey to them specifically where they need to adjust for optimal outcomes.

9. Find out what is important to your employees and let them know what is important to you. The new workforce loves collaboration.

10. Be flexible. That might mean providing flex time, letting employees work from home occasionally or letting them leave work early for a personal matter when appropriate. The flexibility when combined with clear expectations and closely adhered to performance standards can produce very effective and fully engaged employees.

11. Provide training that prepares employees for advancement opportunities as well as training for improved performance in their current position.

12. Provide fair and equitable compensation and benefits. The best and brightest won't be content for long in an organization that pays the CEO thousands of times what employees make.

The Right Environment

Because Generation X and, to an even greater degree, Millennials have gathered their world view and values from video games and a chaotic, unpredictable environment, they intrinsically understand that the idea of constancy is a fictional construct.

In *Understanding the Millennial Mind - A Menace or Amazing*, Millennial expert Scott Degraffenreid sums up the new workforce quite accurately. He says young people have seen so many "truths" and "realities" come and go in their short lives that they have become masters at letting go. "The one thing they believe they can count on is that no one can count on anything forever," Degraffenreid says. This view makes these generations seem cynical and immature to the older, more absolute generations, but Degraffenreid believes this approach gives Millennials an operational awareness that provides huge advantages in the turbulent and unpredictable world in which we find ourselves (Degraffenreid 2008).

The very same factors that lead Generation X and Millennials to walk out the door when they perceive themselves to be in a no-win situation can, when properly directed, create amazingly effective strategists and problem-solvers.

The last half of Generation X and all Millennials have been immersed from birth in the need for a much more pragmatic reality. They have seen first-hand that things don't always work the way they are supposed to and they don't expect anything to work all the time.

Through years of interviewing Millennials, Degraffenreid has found that they tend to depend on something as long as it delivers what they expect, but they don't expect anything to deliver indefinitely. He says that anything these generations choose to accept is generally adopted with a tacit understanding that they will hold onto it as long as it works, but they are quick to abandon anything that is no longer working for them.

This attitude can be a huge problem if leaders fail to take advantage of it, and it can be a real blessing if they do. Because the new generations only hold onto something as long as it works, they are not likely to continue working on a project that is going nowhere for months or years. If something isn't working they are likely to raise lots of red flags which can save organizations untold amounts of time and money.

Of the Millennial generation's pervasive tendency toward impermanence, Degraffenreid suggests that it is both easy and tempting to mis-characterize their behavior as disloyalty. He suggests the behaviors are actually an expression of a "fundamental over-arching loyalty to *what works*." Millennials are not attached to knowing the truth or being right as much as they are committed to things going as well as they possibly can. Their way of ensuring that things turn out is to promptly but not prematurely let go of things that cease to provide optimal outcomes.

Degraffenreid sees Millennials as the new masters of the quick release; a generation that has been quietly perfecting their timing, learning to shift neither too soon nor too late. When the winds of change start blowing, as they often do in today's world, Millennials waste no time looking back or clinging foolishly to a course that can't be effectively steered. Today's generations, especially Millennials, are full of energy, creativity and innovative solutions. Organizations that ignore them will watch their attrition rate continue to skyrocket as customer service ratings plunge.

Leaders who insist that the emerging workforce is "broken" and try to "fix" employees by enforcing rules and increasing oversight will discover they are fighting a losing battle. These generations are "game masters" and if they decide to stay in such an organization it's because they feel compelled to beat those who are trying to control them at their own game or worse, to crash their system.

Leaders that learn to collaborate with, rather than try to control the new generations, will discover that they are smart and adept at the things organizations need to compete in the global markets of today and tomorrow. These generations are capable of quantum leap innovations and incredible process streamlining. They can track, analyze and think in multiple layers. Forming global teams and complex networks is child's play for them.

In today's fast-paced, rapid changing, highly competitive world the ability of the new generations to shift and change easily is really quite beneficial. But the majority of older generation leaders continue to cling to outmoded notions of how things should be and fail to see the value in this new approach. OZ leaders that do see it often fear it and try to control it.

It's time to embrace these generations and learn to work with them in the only way they are going to work. Hoping things will someday be like they once were; that the "youngsters" will someday grow up and start acting like the Traditional or Silent Generations, or even the Boomers, is bound to result in disappointment, frustration, and financial loss. Right now organizations still have options that will impact both their bottom line and corporate relevance, but that will not be true for long.

The reality is that the new workforce lives in a completely different world and plays by completely different rules. Leaders must meet those they wish to lead where they live, not where the leader *wishes* they lived. To expect those we aspire to lead to willingly leave their reality and embrace ours is folly. Organizations that want to attract and keep the best and the brightest will have to meet the new workforce in their own world and, for today's informed generations, that will never be OZ.

To Boards of Directors

In the interest of saving organizations that have become American icons, here's a tip for the Boards of Directors of the old, staid organizations. We hope you are listening.

The primary motivation of many of the leaders running your organizations is not more money, it is power; power that they cling to and strive to maintain through control and domination. Stop throwing money at them and start building a team of Visionary Leaders who can bring *real* power—the power of cooperation—to your organization. If the bottom line is what you are interested in, paying high dollar salaries to power hungry Wizards is *not* the way to improve it. Imagine saving billions of dollars in executive salaries while, at the same time, increasing effectiveness.

The self-proclaimed Wizards will never admit to this. In fact, they will vehemently deny it, but decades of research and experience have clearly demonstrated that team-oriented businesses, where employees are empowered and engaged, and where the salaries of the leaders are not hundreds of times those of the workers, not only have happier, more dedicated and engaged employees, they also *make more money*.

In spite of all the data proving that the new approach both works and is profitable, many corporate leaders continue to choose power, control and domination over making the company more successful.

But, make no mistake, in a hierarchical, command and control culture, employee engagement is low—and getting lower. In a few years employee engagement will be all but non-existent in OZ organizations and the motivation to perform to capacity almost nil. Is that your vision for your organization? If not, now is the time to act.

To Workers Still Looking for a Place to Call Home

Avoid employers who see employees as part of the problem or as interchangeable cogs in a wheel rather than as a means for affecting solutions through cooperation and collaboration.

If you want to know what a company truly values, look at what they do and where they invest their resources, not at what they say.

A company that proudly proclaims to the world that their employees are their greatest asset and that they are an employer of choice, but that has a 30% employee turnover rate with an average tenure of under five years, is deluded.

Talk to the employees who see the reality, not to the interviewers and leaders. You won't get the truth from the officials because they are out of touch with reality and can't see it.

Companies that truly value their employees consider them their greatest asset and it shows. They make it their business to create an environment where employees want to stay. Don't just stop at checking out their sales pitch and the physical environment. These can be clever disguises. Remember, the Wizard is great at pomp and ceremony.

Evidence of their effectiveness (or lack thereof) can better be found in the pace at which the workforce is or is *not* exiting. Places like Google, Southwest Airlines, Intuit and Zappos have almost no voluntary employee turnover. And at Google, Intuit and Zappos most of their employees are Gen Xers and Millennials, which proves that, in the right environment, they are excellent workers who stay put.

Organizations such as these experience such low turnover because they have taken the time to understand their employees and build a culture around the way today's workforce wants to work. These organizations don't just give lip service to putting people first, they really do it. Truly progressive companies are not easy to find right now, but they are well worth the search.

Dorothy: Weren't you frightened?

Wizard of Oz: Frightened? Child you're talking to a man who's laughed in the face of death, sneered at doom and chuckled at catastrophe... I was petrified.

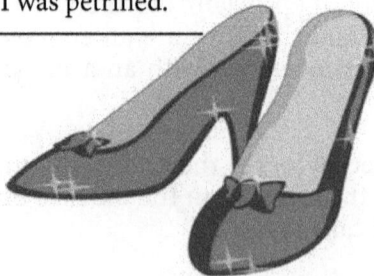

CHAPTER TWENTY-ONE
Homecoming

In the film, Dorothy discovered that all she had to do to get home was click her heels three times and say, "There's no place like home." On the surface it appeared that the ruby slippers created the magic to get Dorothy home and to protect her from all the dangers as she traveled through the Land of Oz. In reality, the abilities attributed to the slippers were inside her all along.

The slippers represent courage and conviction; something today's workforce has plenty of when it comes to getting themselves into a place that feels like home. Like Dorothy, they are quick to leave a place, no matter how fascinating, that doesn't meet their criteria for what "home" should be. They simply keep clicking their heels and reminding themselves that there is "no place like home" and off they go.

If organizations hope to keep these workers, they are going to have to do more than "re-engineer". They will have to re-think, re-design and re-build almost from the ground up. The sterile workplace of yesterday will not hold these employees. Business as usual never did engage many employees, but traditional expectations did hold them. As we have seen, that is no longer true.

Today's workforce is steadily exiting OZ in search of a place that feels like home, and they are relentless in their efforts to find it.

More and more are opting to enter the workforce as independent subcontractors offering their services to the highest bidder. As subcontractors, they are willing to show up and do the job as long as the people they interact with and the environment supports them and makes doing the job pleasant. When that is not the case, they are quickly gone and off to the next "gig". This can be very costly to organizations that don't know how to keep these workers interested and engaged.

A subcontractor arrangement can be good for employers and employees as long as there is some continuity. Unfortunately, where the environment and leadership are perceived as non-supportive, continuity is, and will continue to be, almost non-existent with the younger generations.

For organizations to keep workers as employees or subcontractors, they are going to have to figure out what the workforce they are now inheriting wants, needs and values, and give it to them.

The good news is that what the "Baby Bulge" group wants is what organizations really do need. When you look at the skills most organizations name as critical and compare them to what Generation X and Millennials bring to the table, it becomes apparent that a change in the leadership model and the work environment is merited and will be well worth the effort.

Critical Skills that Employers Seek

Communication - By far, the one skill mentioned most often by employers is the ability to speak, write, and listen effectively. Successful communication and listening skills are critical business skills.

Are today's generations proficient here? In person, no more than any other generation, but via the internet they are unparalleled—and the internet is rapidly becoming the communication tool of choice. If you need effective in-person communication, realize communication is a skill, and skills can be taught provided the employee is first engaged. Before any skill can be learned, engagement must occur. Getting employee buy in must always be the first goal.

What engages Generation X and Millennials? The answer to that question can be summed up in two words; *respect* and *choice.* They want to be respected and they want to respect the company they work for. They are adamant about the need for respect between themselves and their leader. Millennials, especially, expect employers to genuinely care about a greater good beyond financial profit and to convey that, not just to employees, but to the world. Organizations that fail to convey that they are concerned about the greater good will not gain the respect or allegiance of the new workforce.

These generations also want to be both engaged and included in the process of making a positive impact. So show them how the success of your organization will make a positive impact and collaborate with them on how to ensure success. Choice goes beyond collaboration for these generations, however. They also want to be able to decide, at least to some extent, how and when they work. Flex time and performance-based systems are very appealing to them.

Analytical Skills – The ability to assess a situation, see multiple perspectives, gather information as necessary, scrutinize, improve and streamline complex processes, and identify key issues is another often cited set of requirements

Are today's generations proficient here? As a rule, yes. This is one of the benefits of "gaming". Growing up analyzing ways to get from level to level in fast-paced video games has given Gen Xers and Millennials an advantage in seeing things from multiple perspectives and in finding ways to identify roadblocks, improve strategies and streamline complex processes.

Computer/Technical Literacy – Almost all jobs now require at least a basic understanding of computer hardware and software, word processing, spreadsheet creation, and e-mail communication. Computer-literate workers with extensive proficiency covering a wide variety of applications are highly prized today.

There is no question in anyone's mind that the younger generations are proficient here. They practically teethed on computers and video controllers.

Flexibility, Adaptability and Multitasking – As organizations try to adjust to the rapidly changing marketplace, having employees with the ability to manage multiple assignments and tasks, set priorities, and adapt to changing conditions and work assignments is critical to organizational success.

The younger generations are highly proficient here. They grew up in a fast-paced world in which their mental, emotional, and sometimes physical survival depended on how well they could flex and adapt.

As to managing multiple assignments, Gen Xers and Millennials are not just able, they actually expect life to proceed that way. It's why we see news briefs streaming across the bottom of the television screen when we watch newscasts these days. These generations become bored when there are not lots of things going on. Their ease with multi-tasking is another of the benefits of "gaming".

Interpersonal Abilities – The ability to relate to coworkers is an essential ability given the amount of time people spend at work each day. Interpersonal skills go beyond communication, though they are certainly part of this skill set. Interpersonal skills also include the ability to inspire others to participate, to manage one's own emotions and keep conflict with co-workers at a minimum.

As with communication skills, training to improve interpersonal skills may be necessary for a good percentage of Gen Xers and Millennials, but probably not a lot more than would be beneficial to any generation. Few people have had sufficient training in social skills, yet good social and interpersonal skills are key to employee engagement.

Multicultural Sensitivity/Awareness – As we move into a global arena, this has become a critically important issue in the workplace. Employees are expected, even required to demonstrate sensitivity and awareness to other people and cultures today.

The good news is that Generation X and Millennials grew up in a multicultural world. Not only have they been exposed to the world through the media all their lives, they have been on the internet chatting all over the world and happily learning about other cultures and other ways of life. Cultural sensitivity and the ability to connect with diverse people is second nature to many of them.

Leadership/Management Skills – Organizations are continually looking for goal-driven leaders who can maintain a productive climate and effectively inspire, motivate, mobilize, and coach employees to high performance standards. Yet many organizations still insist on recruiting OZ style leaders.

There is a pervasive and very mistaken notion that the most valuable leaders are primarily focused on "get it done" and "get it right" initiatives. Yet that is not what studies of the best leaders suggest, and it is certainly not what will work with today's generations.

Leadership skills, like communication, are *learned* skills for the most part and there are just as many people among the Generation X and Millennial generations with natural leadership talents waiting to be developed as there has ever been in any generation.

Getting and Keeping the Best and Brightest

In order for organizations to remain attractive to the best and brightest workers—an absolute necessity as the imminent departure of Baby Boomers creates a huge void—they must begin to address the valid concerns and expectations of Generation X and Millennial workers while, at the same time, complying with the larger responsibilities of corporate America.

So what will achieve that grand goal? What are Generation X and Millennials looking for? What will keep the best and the brightest among these generations in one place giving a full measure of their skills and abilities? What exactly does a workplace "home" look like? And can organizations create such an environment without completely compromising their own values and needs? We believe that the answer is a resounding "yes!" And we have seen a lot of evidence to back up that belief.

What Generation X and Millennials consider "home" was covered in part in chapter 18 (There's No Place Like Home), but a recap here will provide the makings of a blueprint for designing a workplace that will keep the employees of today and tomorrow engaged, productive and performing at peak levels.

Develop and Convey a Social Conscience

The newest generations, especially Millennials, have long been criticized as "entitled" generations used to getting what they want, when they want it. However, research on Millennials tells a different story. According to a recent study, 61% of this generation said they felt personally responsible for making a difference in the world and more than 72% have taken it upon themselves to educate family and friends on social and environmental causes (Cone and AMP Insights 2006).

Millennials are intent on making the world a better place, and, in turn, they expect others, including their employers, to do the same. You can get great things from Millennials and Generation X by finding ways to help them turn their personal commitment to the social good into a positive work experience.

Members of these generations are eager to be a part of innovative companies that leverage their resources to make a significant impact through corporate social responsibility. Know your company's vision, mission and purpose and regularly convey them to your employees. If your current mission is "exceptional customer service," you need to rethink it. That has no real meaning to your employees. Look deeper. How will your customers actually benefit from what you provide? That is what you want to convey.

For example: a manufacturer of telephone equipment might convey that their mission is to provide their customers with freedom from worry by ensuring that they have telephone equipment that the customer can absolutely depend upon when they need to reach someone or get help. Employees can visualize a stranded motorist or an elderly citizen being aided by a dependable phone in a time of need and feel moved by that. They can't feel anything about "exceptional customer service."

Be Honest and Up Front About Your Social Responsibility Practices

Remember; these generations have grown up in the shadow of Enron and the corruption of once revered companies like Arthur Andersen. They have seen the irresponsible way in which British Petroleum handled the gulf oil disaster and Wall Street banks handled the bailout funds.

Organizations must find ways to effectively counter the negative stereotypes and distrust these generations have for almost any kind of establishment. A concerted effort toward best practices in corporate social responsibility is not enough. To score with the newer generations you need to demonstrate pride and dedication to what your company stands for and actually does. Don't try to do more in the area of social responsibility than makes sense given your business objectives and certainly do not claim to be doing more than you actually are. Your employees will see right through it and you will lose their respect and their loyalty.

Develop and Convey an Environmental Conscience

Generation X and Millennials were introduced to the importance of protecting their environment in grade school. They have grown up hearing about endangered species and melting ice caps. As adults, they believe that wise environmental practices are vital to sustaining the world.

To keep these generations engaged and committed to your organization, you must demonstrate that you too are environmentally aware and committed to a sustainable environment. The idea of an organization damaging the environment in the name of money is grossly distasteful to these generations.

Leverage what you are already doing for the environment by being vocal about it. For example, hotels ask guests to reuse their towels to cut down on water waste and the dumping of detergents into the water system. Though it could be argued that the hotels are simply trying to cut their overhead costs, the request is presented as an environmentally friendly move. That is also true and they have capitalized on that fact.

Adopt Green Practices

Adopting "green" practices internally is something else that is important to the new workforce and this practice can save you money too. Green products, such as recycled paper and refilled ink cartridges, have become increasingly easy to use and are often less expensive to buy. Low-energy appliances and compact fluorescent light bulbs are also money savers. If you use these measures, let your employees know. It's important to them and will build loyalty for you.

Encourage Innovation

In today's fast changing world you must be continually innovating to keep up. By creating an environment and systems that minimize costly mistakes while allowing for rapid, and sometimes radical change, you will not only be encouraging innovation and positive change, you will better hold the interest of the new generations who love adapting to new trends, and will be way ahead of the game.

Build a Responsible Brand Identity

Today's generations make it a point to buy from companies that are taking steps to be socially and environmentally conscious according to a survey conducted by Alloy Media & Marketing Group. These generations actively promote the products and services of such companies and these are the companies they seek to work for.

In the Cone, Inc. study cited on page 173, nearly half of the Millennials surveyed reported that they would not buy a product from a company with a poor social reputation. If they won't even buy products from a company they don't respect, it's hard to imagine that they would go to work for one and perform well.

Ask and Listen

The newer generations are poised to make a huge impact on the way organizations are run and they know it. Organizational leaders had better know it too. The best way to know what your employees want, need, and expect is to ASK them. But *do not ask if you don't plan to listen and make the indicated changes.* We have seen employees mutiny company-wide as a result of management doing surveys to solicit employee feedback and then ignoring the data.

Develop a Deeper Awareness of Personal Traits

The relentless search for top talent and the hemorrhaging of time and money experienced by so many organizations in their efforts to build an effective workforce is evidence that the methods currently being used by these organizations are *not* working. One reason is that these methods fail to uncover the most critical aspects of the people being hired, promoted and placed. While typical methods, such as resume' and background checks can provide some indication of an individual's work ethic and how he or she typically behaves, they do not necessarily provide clear indicators of what was required for those past behaviors to emerge, or what it will take to have them continue.

It is not uncommon for an organization to hire an individual that, on paper, looks like a perfect fit only to have that person fail miserably within months of being hired, or for what starts out as a star performer to quickly move to a place of disillusionment and burnout and leave after a year or so. The reason these kinds of things happen so regularly is that the most critical elements for success cannot be seen, measured or predicted from the surface. Employers need to look deeper.

Develop a Clear Awareness of Generational Values

Baby Boomers tend to see feedback as telling people exactly what they are doing wrong and what to do to correct it. Gen Xers and Millennials want feedback that is framed with positive reinforcement. Though not always positive, they typically got plenty of feedback from their parents and from politically correct teachers, so that is the kind of interaction they are accustomed to and expect.

Where Baby Boomers and every generation before them valued, or at least gave lip service to, teamwork, Gen Xers and Millennials embrace more individualized work. Though they are highly social electronically and even in social settings, they are not as comfortable giving up their autonomy to work in teams. They prefer to spend their time on things that are meaningful to them personally rather than on what the team as a whole may want. In-person situations do not afford them the level of control they have in the electronic world where they can just disconnect from someone they are not relating to.

One Millennial Gina interviewed reported that he is hesitant to work in teams only because past experience with teams convinced him that he could be more effective outside a team environment. He said he would love to work in teams if they could be counted upon to be trustworthy and to perform well. Yet he also stated that he doesn't want to be judged based on the lack of performance of someone else. "I want to stand on my own merit," he explained. "I like working with other people, but I don't want to be graded on their performance."

For Millennials to be comfortable working in teams, team dynamics are going to have to shift. Millennials are willing to collaborate with others, it seems, as long as they are evaluated as individuals.

Electronically, Millennials can instantly break the connection and be in their own private space, and that's often the way they prefer it. This has added to their reluctance to work with people they view as difficult, untrustworthy or non-performing.

Throw Out the Myths

Myth #1: Younger generations have no work ethic.

Reality: The younger generations have a self-actualizing work ethic. They want their work to be meaningful and, when it is, they are dedicated workers intent on completing tasks such that they will personally be proud of the result. Although they may not yet know to look around and see what needs to be done next, they are more than willing to do the work they are assigned. They want clarity as to what their job entails and its value. When they have that, they will figure out the best and fastest way to complete the task and get to it. Once finished, they consider themselves done and simply wait for the next assignment. And while they wait, they spend their time on personally enjoyable activities. Older workers see this as goofing off where the younger ones see it as a useful expenditure of time. A key difference between older and younger generations is that older generations tend to work in day-long blocks of time where the younger generations work from project to project.

Myth #2: Younger generations won't put in the hours to get ahead.

Reality: They are willing to put in the time necessary to get the job done; but have little interest in simply clocking time. Where older generations tend to consider time as something to invest for future benefit, the younger generations view it as a valuable currency that should be used wisely *today* and not wasted or spent on future plans that may or may not pan out. They want to get the job done and then put it behind them so they can enjoy their life. The emerging workforce is not willing to be slaves to an organization in order to get ahead as past generations were, but organizations that provide a work/life balance will find that the younger generations are highly dedicated workers.

Myth #3: Younger generations have no respect for authority.

Reality: They have great respect for *effective* and *caring* leaders and are extremely loyal to those who earn their trust and respect. As a rule, they do not respect authority just because it is built into the hierarchy. For the younger generations, every ounce of respect must be earned and no loyalty is forthcoming until it is. For those who bother to earn it, it is given deeply.

Myth #4: Younger generations don't want to grow up.

Reality: It is true that the younger generations tend to delay adulthood. They are leaving home, getting married, having children and facing the "real world" much later than previous generations did. There are several reasons for this. The main one is that the world is a lot scarier than it once was. Things change at a break-neck speed and nothing is certain. When the ship we are to navigate life in is moving over choppy waters, it takes longer to develop sturdy "sea legs." These generations really want those "sea legs" though. It is why they are so keen on personal development and training initiatives. Be willing to provide them with the training and development they want and need. Your investment will not be wasted.

Myth #5: Younger generations are impossible to motivate.

Reality: The younger generations are bright and alert. Early on they saw the toll their Boomer parents, and they as children, paid as a result of the long hours their parents worked and they have no desire to follow in their parent's footsteps. The younger generations don't view the corporate ladder as something to aspire to climb. They look at it and think, "There must be a better way."

The reason organizations are having such a difficult time motivating the younger generations is because they are holding up the wrong things as enticements. The younger generations are not motivated by money or position or clout. They couldn't care less about the corporate ladder. They want equality and collaboration and meaning. They want to be heard and included in decision making. They want to use their brains and talents for more than just mindless compliance.

If you wonder whether the younger generations can be consistently motivated to exceptional levels of performance just take a look at Google. See what that company has accomplished in a few short years. See what it continues to accomplish. And, while you are at it, see what they are doing. Then do that. If you do, motivating your younger employees will never be a problem.

Myth #6: Younger generations are not loyal to their employers.

Reality: Again, take a look at Google. Their employees are fiercely loyal. The reason the younger generations leave most organizations at such alarming rates is because they are completely immersed in a deeply pragmatic reality. They have seen firsthand that things work until they don't, and they are not inclined to depend on something that is clearly not working. This approach is not disloyalty, though it is both easy and tempting to assume as much. It is in fact, deep loyalty to a principle—to what works. They are committed to making things go as well as they possibly can, and sometimes that means letting go of things that are not providing optimal outcomes.

The younger generations have spent years perfecting their timing, learning to shift at just the right time—to make their moves neither too soon nor too late. They are certain that the only thing they can count on is that things will change and these generations waste no time looking back or foolishly clinging to a course that can't be successfully navigated. These really are excellent skills and every organization should be embracing them. After all, it isn't just the younger generations that must successfully navigate the world we have created.

Know What is Really at Stake

The emergence of the new era ushered in mostly by the Millennial mindset has far greater implications than just the impact on an organization's workforce. It will greatly impact the face of consumerism too. Not only can organizations no longer lead the way they used to, they cannot afford to market or even *think* the way they used to.

Unlike their parents, Millennials are not conspicuous consumers except in electronics, and are not likely to ever move in that direction. The economic conditions that exist today and the cost of bailing us out of the recession that hit in 2008 has created conditions that will keep the newer generations spending carefully—if not cautiously—for many years to come; probably for an entire lifetime as happened with those who experienced the Great Depression.

Right now much of the population is marching to the beat of a new and different drummer when it comes to spending. Some may return to old spending habits when the economy gets better, but organizations that depend on that are likely to find themselves in deep trouble down the road.

Spending habits have shifted to some extent across the board affecting all generations, and spending is not likely to return to its pre-2008 level in our lifetimes. There has been a measurable shift away from conspicuous consumption that is being felt in every industry, even the once immune high end markets. Luxury buying has dropped off significantly according to reports from high end retailers such as Neiman Marcus and Saks. So it's safe to assume that, if even the most affluent are rethinking spending, the overall trend will be in that direction.

Frivolous spending may not be dead, but it sure is severely weakened. To survive and thrive in the world we now live in, and in the foreseeable future, organizations must make sure they provide a solid reason for every product and service they offer—not just to the consumer, but also to the employees they hope to keep engaged and productive.

Training

Long before the term "coaching" expanded beyond sports and entertainment arenas and entered organizations, Gina and I were training in a way that is now considered group coaching. We called the process segmented training because the term "coaching" had not yet entered the world of business. But as trainers coming from a psychological background, we quickly realized that typical training methods did not get good results. They pushed people to learn in ways that are not conducive to learning, so we developed methods for teaching the way people best learn; experientially and in easily digestible chunks.

We wanted to incorporate all five steps for learning; impact, repetition, utilization, internalization and reinforcement, and to do that we held students accountable for doing the assignments we gave them—assignments performed in real world scenarios. We took another step not then typical to training but now familiar to coaches, that of making sure there was complete buy-in from participants before even attempting to begin the teaching process.

Benjamin Franklin wrote, "*Tell me and I forget. Teach me and I remember. Involve me and I learn.*" For learning to occur, employees must be involved. If they are disengaged, they are not involved and will not learn no matter how good the training program might be. The group coaching model is by far the best learning model, especially for the newer generations.

The Bottom Line

The bottom line is that today's workforce is like no other. They have seen behind the curtain and there is no going back. Employers that meet them where they live will be amazed at their ability and willingness to help the organization achieve its goals. Employers that try to force them to fit their model of what the workplace "should" be like should fully expect employee push-back and high and persistent turnover rates.

The new workforce is steadily exiting OZ and will continue to do so in their quest to find a place to call home. Find out what that looks like to them and provide it.

If you do, you will have an organization filled with engaged, dedicated, high performance employees that are actively contributing to the bottom line and the overall well-being of the organization; employees who are perfectly suited to the demands of today and who are more than happy to stay put and help your organization succeed.

The new workforce is actively searching and would love to find a place to land, but it has to be the right place. They are not willing to settle. It's a refrain we regularly hear from them. Perhaps more than any other generation, they understand that the workplace is their second home and it needs to be a good fit. Provide the fit and you will have all the bright, dedicated workers you will ever need. And they won't be jumping ship every few years either because, like Dorothy, these generations are certain that *there is no place like home.*

About the Authors

Sherry Buffington, PhD is an internationally recognized authority on performance, motivation, leadership and organizational effectiveness. She is a pioneer in the field of developmental assessments and performance improvement at both personal and professional levels. Dr. Buffington is president and CEO of NaviCore International, Inc., a research and development firm focused on behavioral analysis and performance optimization.

She is the originator and co-developer of the highly acclaimed *CORE Multidimensional Awareness Profile* and the *CORE Personal Effectiveness Profile*, author of several books including *The 7 Essentials for Lasting Success, Who's Got the Compass?... I Think I'm Lost!, The Productivity Path, One Great Idea, The Law of Abundance,* and *Communicate to Connect,* and has developed curriculum for numerous adult training programs.

Dr. Buffington has over 30 years of experience helping organizational leaders improve outcomes and maximize performance and productivity. As an avid researcher, assessment developer, organizational consultant, trainer, and presenter in the areas of leadership, employee effectiveness, communication, and team dynamics she brings a unique perspective to organizations and a set of skills that result in significant and measurable improvements, maximum productivity and increased profits. Her work has contributed to the transformation of hundreds of organizations and many thousands of individual lives and relationships.

Her clients range from individual coaches and therapists to Fortune 100 corporations.

To learn more or to book Sherry for a speaking, training or coaching engagement, visit our website at www.exitingoz.com

Gina Morgan, CMCC, is a personal and executive coach, certified Master CORE analyst, trainer and author. Her direct approach coupled with her ability to truly connect with her clients allows her to get to core issues rapidly and help clients overcome old conditioned patterns and roadblocks that have been preventing them from achieving their desired outcomes personally and professionally.

Gina is also a certified grief recovery counselor which gives her a unique ability to tap into and heal pain points that may be affecting productivity and outcomes. She is an expert in the areas of leadership, inter-personal effectiveness, change management, communication, diplomacy, stress management, interpersonal dynamics, and team effectiveness.

Gina has over 20 years of experience helping clients develop their natural strengths, improve communications, develop greater levels of EQ, improve relationship outcomes and maximize personal productivity. She has developed curriculum for numerous adult training programs as well as editing and curriculum services used by several community colleges and universities.

Gina is vice-president of NaviCore International, Inc. and co-developer of the highly acclaimed CORE Multidimensional Awareness Profile and the CORE Personal Effectiveness Profile. Her clients range from individual coaches and therapists to Fortune 100 corporations.

To learn more or to book Gina for a speaking, training or coaching engagement, visit our website at www.exitingoz.com

Julie Overholt, PCC is an internationally recognized Executive Coach to leaders of Fortune 100 companies. Her passion for working with leaders includes executive re-invention to help leaders align their strengths to the demanding issues that impact their organization's sustainability and profitability.

With over 25 years of experience in talent development and career consulting, Julie's emerging interest is helping organizations evolve their mission and values into global initiatives that enhance their impact in the world profitably and socially.

Credentialed as a Professional Certified Coach through the International Coach Federation in 1996, Julie is considered a pioneer in the profession of business coaching. She is a graduate of Coach University and affiliated with the Graduate School of Coaching, Legacy Leadership Institute and Target Training, International. She has a BA in Speech from Augustana College in Rock Island, Illinois. Julie is also a Certified Professional Behavioral Analyst and CORE trained analyst.

Julie has been used as an expert resource for Entrepreneur Magazine, Men's Health, Ft. Worth Star Telegram, numerous technology magazines, print and media outlets across the United States.

To learn more or to book Julie for a speaking, training or coaching engagement, visit our website at www.exitingoz.com

Dr. Glen Earl is an expert in Leadership Development, Organizational Effectiveness and Employee Engagement with 20 years experience as a business psychologist. His experience as an employee and as a consultant to thousands of employees in dozens of organizations in 12 countries has given Dr. Earl a clear understanding of the challenges of the multi-generational workforce and the organizational culture needed to sustain long term organizational success. As a successful author and speaker Dr. Earl is an engaging, entertaining and enthusiastic keynote speaker and presenter on topical issues that affect people both at work and at home.

Dr. Earl's philosophy is that of balanced living; a concept dear to the hearts of today's generations, but certainly not a new one. He believes that to live the best possible life we need mental, physical, spiritual, emotional, intellectual, and economic health. His focus is on providing the means to achieve these to anyone ready to make a significant and positive change in their outcomes. Dr. Earl holds a MA and Ph.D. in Organization Psychology from Alliant International University, Los Angeles, CA, a MS in Family Relations from Eastern Michigan University, and a B.S. in Child Development from the University of Utah in Salt Lake City, UT.

To learn more or to book Glen for a speaking, training or coaching engagement, visit our website at www.exitingoz.com

Bibliography

Alloy Media & Marketing Group. *Social Responsibility*. 2008. <www.alloymarketing.com/investor_relations/.../080804a_alloy.doc>

Bardwick, Judith. *In Praise of Good Business: How Optimizing Risk Rewards Both Your Bottom Line and Your People*. New Jersey: Wiley, 1998.

Baum, Frank. *The Wonderful Wizard of Oz*. Chicago: George M. Hill Company, 1900.

Chao, Georgia T. and Philip P. Gardner. *The Important Characteristics of Early Career Jobs: What Do Young Adults Want*. East Lansing, MI: Michigan State University, 2007.

Clifton, James K. *Employee Engagement: A Leading Indicator of Financial Performance*. Gallup, Inc. <http://www.gallup.com/consulting/52/Employee-Engagement.aspx>

Cloutier, George. *Profits Aren't Everything, They're the Only Thing*. New York: HarperCollins, 2009.

Collins, Jim. *Good to Great*. New York: HarperCollins, 2001.

Cone Inc. with AMP Agency. *Millennial Generation: Pro-Social and Empowered to Change the World*. 2006. <www.coneinc.com/.../2006_cone_millennial_cause_study_white_paper.pdf>

Covey, Stephen M.R. *The Speed of Trust*. New York: The Free Press, 2006.

Croft-Baker, Nancy. "Eight Companies Keep E-learning from E-scaping." *New Corporate University Review*. March/April 2001.

Degraffenreid, Scott. *Understanding the Millennial Mind - A Menace or Amazing*. 2008. < http://bigbusinesszoo.com/wp-content/uploads/2010/11/Understanding_the_Millennial_Mind_free_eBook1.pdf>

Entrepreneur.com. "Sirota Survey Intelligence." *Human Resource Statistics*. March 13, 2006. <www.entrepreneur.com/encyclopedia/businessstatistics/article81978.html>

Franklin, Benjamin. Quote. <http://thinkexist.com/quotation/tell_me_and_i_forget-teach_me_and_i_remember/154986.html>

Frauenheim, Ed. "Libby's Life in HR – So Far." *Workforce Management.* May 19, 2008. <http://www.workforce.com/section/hr-management/feature/libbys-life-hr-so-far/index.html>

Goleman, Daniel. *Emotional Intelligence: Why It Can Matter More Than IQ.* New York: Bantam, 1995.

Huffington, Arianna. "Move Your Money." T*he Huffington Post.* 2010. <http://www.huffingtonpost.com/arianna-huffington/move-your-money-a-new-yea_b_406022.html>

Johnson, Mike. *The New Rules of Engagement: Life-work Balance and Employee Commitment.* London: CIPD Enterprises, 2004.

Kenny, Bernadette. "The Coming Crises in Employee Turnover." *Forbes Magazine.* April 25, 2007.

Kotter, John P. and James L. Heskett. *Corporate Culture and Performance.* New York: The Free Press, 1992.

Marchman, Jim. T*he Last Western Flyer: The Western Auto Century.* Blacksburg, VA: Marchman, 2004.

McGregor, Douglas. *The Human Side of Enterprise.* New York: McGraw Hill, 1960.

Moore, Angela. "J.C. Penney fires COO Catherine West." *Market Watch: The New York Times.* December, 2006.

Peter, Laurence J. *The Peter Principle.* New York: HarperCollins, 1969.

Peters, Tom & Robert Waterman. *In Search of Excellence.* Clayton, VIC: Warner Books, 1982.

Roberto, Michael. "How to Avoid Becoming the Isolated Executive." *Harvard Business Review.* March 13, 2008.

Wheatley, Margaret. *Leadership and the New Science: Discovering Order in a Chaotic World.* San Francisco, CA: Berret-Koehler, 2009.

Whitney, Kellye. "ROI Controversy Rooted in Expectations." *Chief Learning Officer.* September 13, 2006.

Zielinski, Dave. *The Lie of Online Learning.* Journal. February, 2000.

References to *The Wizard of OZ* film are in reference to the 1939 Metro-Goldwyn-Mayer film directed by Victor Fleming from a script written by Noel Langley, Florence Ryerson and Edgar Allan Woolf. The film was adapted from *The Wonderful Wizard of Oz* by L. Frank Baum and starred Judy Garland, Ray Bolger, Jack Haley, Bert Lahr and Frank Morgan.

The illustrations in this book, other than those created by Sherry Buffington, are provided courtesy of EducationalColoringPages.com and ColoringPagesforKids.info

Index